EXPEC

JESUS

EXPECTING JESUS

Advent reflections and prayers for personal and group use

MARTYN DAY

First published in 2000 by
KEVIN MAYHEW LTD
Buxhall
Stowmarket
Suffolk IP14 3BW

0 1 2 3 4 5 6 7 8 9

ISBN 1 84003 607 9
Catalogue No 1500379

Cover design by Jonathan Stroulger
incorporating elements of an original painting by Honor Day

Edited by Helen Elliot
Typeset by Elisabeth Bates
Printed and bound in Great Britain

. . . and she gave birth to her firstborn, a son.
(Luke 2:7)

This book is dedicated to Thomas, my firstborn, and to Honor, my beautiful wife who gave him birth. You have both helped me to see Christmas in deeper ways.

ABOUT THE AUTHOR

Martyn Day is the author of *Beyond Easter* (SPCK). Formerly the administrator for the evangelist J. John, he continues to work in administration in the secular world. He and his family worship at St Nicholas', Nottingham, where he is on the preaching team. Martyn Day is married to Honor and they have a son, Thomas.

CONTENTS

ACKNOWLEDGEMENTS

Writing this book has at times felt like being pregnant! From conception to birth there have been ups and downs and there are various people who have given me support and encouragement during this time whom I would now like to thank.

In the early stages of the project, David Martin and Mike Abel allowed me access to their computers to get the first faltering pages down on paper. Thank you both for your generosity of spirit. Thanks also to Ralph and Helen Goldenberg and Angela Abel for test-running the material. Your comments and insights were extremely helpful. I appreciate your honesty and your encouragement. I also wish to express my appreciation to my mother and father for proofreading the manuscript. Thank you for the time you gave to do this task so thoroughly. No wayward apostrophe escapes your gaze!

Special thanks to my wife Honor, whose support is sure and whose love is strong. Thank you for all your inspiration along the way and for believing in this project as much as I have. Your medical expertise kept the text accurate and provided interesting insights. Never have your embryology textbooks been so useful! Special thanks for the stunning painting which provided the inspiration for the front cover.

Final thanks to my son Thomas, whose smile always puts life in perspective at the end of the day. Whenever I hold you, I am awed that once upon a time the God of heaven and earth chose to make himself as small as you.

INTRODUCTION

'You, my God, are the most hidden from us,
and yet the most present among us.' St Augustine

Emmanuel – 'God is with us' – is one of the most beautiful words in the language of Christmas. Encapsulating one of God's greatest promises to us, it comes to fulfil the deep need we have for companionship, a need built into all of us by God himself since Adam first breathed Eden's air.

Down the centuries the promise of his presence has been repeatedly whispered from within scrolls of ancient parchment. Among the nomadic Israelites wandering in an inhospitable wilderness with no permanent home in sight, God chose to dwell in the tabernacle, saying these words: 'I will put my dwelling place among you and I will not abhor you. I will walk among you and be your God, and you will be my people' (Leviticus 26:11-12).

To the next generation of Israelites, now facing the prospect of driving out powerful nations to lay claim to the Promised Land, God spoke once more, this time through Moses: 'Do not be terrified by them, for the Lord your God, who is among you, is a great and awesome God' (Deuteronomy 7:21).

Many years later God had not forgotten that promise. To the ears of the Israelites, returning from exile in Babylon after 70 years of seeming rejection from God, his words through the prophet Haggai must have been as sweet as they were simple: 'I am with you' (Haggai 1:13, 2:4).

500 years after this the same message came again: 'Greetings, you who are highly favoured! The Lord is with you' (Luke 1:28). This time the words came from the angel Gabriel to an ordinary Jewish girl called Mary. Those words signalled the beginning of the very first Advent, nine months of expectancy for Mary and Joseph as they waited for the birth of the Messiah. This was God's ultimate way of being Emmanuel: not laying aside his deity, yet still fully embracing our humanity. In the person of Jesus Christ, God allowed us the unique opportunity to see, hear

and touch him. 'That which was from the beginning, which we have heard, which we have seen with our eyes, which we have looked at and our hands have touched – this we proclaim concerning the Word of life' (1 John 1:1) is how the Apostle John struggled to convey verbally the mystery of God incarnate.

Can we learn anything from the experiences of Mary and Joseph that first Advent? I believe so. Throughout the nine months of Mary's pregnancy, they were learning valuable lessons about the God who had chosen, quite literally, to be right with them all the time. In the foetal Christ God was there in their midst, granting them a foretaste of what it means for him to be Emmanuel.

There have been times in my life when I have inwardly cried, 'Lord, are you really there?', times when I may have been facing fears or disappointments, illness or pain. Was God still there when times were hard? Weren't my difficulties the very proof that he had abandoned me? Sometimes I have felt like the Psalmist who wrote: 'Why do you hide yourself in times of trouble?' (Psalm 10:1).

Such questions have drawn me back to that first Advent. For the experiences of Mary and Joseph at that time are not so far removed from my own: hopes for the future, inadequacies in the present, fears and concerns. In the unborn Christ God was right there with them in all their circumstances. By studying their example I am powerfully persuaded that God is with us too.

So come with me and relive that first Advent, from the day of Annunciation to the moment when, in a Bethlehem stable, God first looked on the world through human eyes. We will follow Mary and Joseph's story, observing them at different moments during those nine months and contemplating some of what they would have experienced. Through this journey, combining historical truth and imagination springing from it, I hope that you, like me, will learn to appreciate more fully the God who is Emmanuel.

For each day of December there is a passage of scripture chosen to focus our thoughts, three sections of reflection and a prayer. This book provides only a framework; always remember that the final Word on Christmas is the promised Saviour himself. Ask him to meet with you each day.

Expecting Jesus. That is what this book is about. Mary and Joseph are our guides. Not only did they expect Jesus in the physical sense, but they are also forerunners of all who at any time have looked, with expectant hearts, for the Saviour to be close. We cannot necessarily expect the daily demands upon our lives to be pushed further away, but we can expect to know the Saviour coming close.

My prayer is that this Christmas you will find that the God who sometimes seems so hidden comes a little closer, not because he's ever been distant, but because instead you will discover just how close he really is.

DISCUSSION MATERIAL

At the end of each of the book's four sections you will find discussion material suitable for those wishing to use the themes of the book as a four-part series for Advent and the New Year. Each block of discussion questions begins with a short paragraph summarising the topics covered in the book up to that point. These correspond with the events in the three trimesters of Mary's pregnancy, with one post-Christmas section.

Each group session could involve the use of any of the Bible passages quoted in the book. Sections of the daily reflections could also be read out as springboards for discussion. The group material has been written so that those using the book on an individual basis will further benefit by discussing the issues raised in a group setting. The questions may also be used for further personal reflection by those reading the book only on an individual basis. Each set of questions is based around the topics discussed in the 31 sections/days of the book.

FIRST TRIMESTER
1-8 DECEMBER

1 DECEMBER

THE GOD OF NO LIMITS

Reading: Luke 1:26-38

Mary could not remember how long she sat motionless after Gabriel had gone, basking in the warmth which his presence had brought. In the silence which followed the angel's departure, the pounding of her own heart echoed like thunder within her. For a time it was all she was conscious of. Then, quite slowly, she became aware of her surroundings again.

Had she really said, 'May it be to me as you have said'? For a moment she struggled to believe those words had been hers. Her mind was far from an ocean of calm. To be more honest, questions like threatening waves were already being whipped up by the wind of change. 'Can this really be true? What do I tell Joseph? Will he believe me? Will he disown me? What about everyone else?' With reverence her hand came to rest on her abdomen as a further question rose in her mind: 'And am I pregnant right now?' But even as she asked it, she already knew the answer. Deep within her she knew she felt different. She could not deny it. Her body, so human, had been entrusted with a gift so holy. Something of heaven had touched her. Despite her questions, a quiet acceptance of the ways of God had found a home within her.

And so had God himself.

Near where I live is an army barracks. Dominating the main gate is a sign which reads, 'Prohibited Place'. It is made clear to all who come near that this is a place of restricted access where some people are not welcome.

Mary could have chosen to make her womb a 'prohibited place' for the Son of God. She could have resolved to shun his presence within her. She could have refused to co-operate with the responsibility entrusted to her by Gabriel.

Mary would have had good reason to think this way. The idea of the Messiah being born to a lowly village girl would not have been predicted by most Jews of that time. The very thought of God himself entering the world in this fashion was far removed from their minds. What Mary didn't realise then was that God was simply starting his earthly life in Jesus as he meant to go on. Even as the embryonic Christ, hidden in the secret place of Mary's womb, God was exploding people's expectations of where he should be and what he should do. And this pattern was to continue throughout Jesus' life.

- You would never have expected God in a womb.
- You would never have expected God to mingle with sinners on the earth.
- You would never have expected God on a cross.

Yet each represented an essential facet of his plan of salvation in Christ.

I am challenged by the example of Mary, who allowed God to enter her very womb to fulfil his purposes. She did not put up any barriers to deny God entry. Yet how many times have I done just that with different areas of my life?

It also makes me think of times in my life which I have consciously or unconsciously written off as being ones in which God was not interested. Maybe it was a failure from which I felt nothing could be salvaged, or a disappointment from whose ashes I believed no encouragement could rise. Perhaps it was a fear which still imprisons me and I've reasoned there can be no key to unlock the door.

Mary's example teaches us that there is no place in our lives where we cannot welcome God's Spirit to strengthen, encourage and guide. There is no such thing as a 'no-go' area for him. He is the God who goes where we might not expect him to. The only places that are prohibited for him are the ones in our lives which we deliberately choose to make so. God will not force himself upon us, but he wants to teach us that he can be close in every circumstance.

That's the lesson Mary came to appreciate that first time she knew she was pregnant. She realised that she was not alone, but that someone was with her at each moment of the day and night. She could choose to ignore the presence of the unborn Christ within her, but it would not change the fact that he was there.

We may be facing difficult circumstances which make us feel either that God is not close or that he cannot come close. Take heart, for the angel Gabriel's words of Annunciation can help us, if we will only let them: 'The Lord is with you.' There are no conditions attached to this statement; it's just a plain fact, standing firm in all circumstances. And the one with the eyes to see, who looks to that truth, will discover that they are not alone, whatever their situation. In these Advent days to come, let us be open to learning more of this great truth. For otherwise we will look back on our different circumstances and only realise with hindsight that Jesus was right there all the time.

Prayer

O come, O come, Emmanuel,
and help me to open up my life to you.
Your hand is at the door;
only my will unlocks the latch.
Help me to realise you are ready and able to enter
even those areas of my life I believe you would shun,
that with hands of love and tenderness
you can begin to dismantle the barriers of fear, pain and failure
with which I have prohibited your entry.
This Christmas, teach me to welcome you afresh
and increase my expectations of how close you can be.
Amen.

2 DECEMBER

WHEN THINGS DON'T MAKE SENSE

Reading: Matthew 1:18-24

Joseph was struggling. His mind had been scrambled by Mary's news, leaving a jumbled heap of contradictory thoughts which, when viewed together, made little sense. Joseph had always considered himself to be an active thinker, but he could not remember a time like this, when only sleep graciously granted rest to his mind, and then only through sheer exhaustion.

An uncontrollable see-saw of emotions pivoted inside Joseph's mind, setting love against loyalty in a cruel struggle for his affections. Love for Mary versus loyalty to the law. The prospect of this duel filled Joseph with utter dismay, for whichever side triumphed, the loss of the other would be grievous to him.

He loved Mary deeply, but he had to look at the facts of the case: Messiah or not, Mary was pregnant out of wedlock. This was not how things were meant to be. Joseph thought he had got his life in order. He'd had hopes for his forthcoming marriage. Now he was seeing them disappear in a quagmire of social disgrace. The law cried for Mary's blood, but Joseph's agony persisted because this was not a clear-cut case. Despite her circumstances, Mary had not been unfaithful. But how would anyone else believe them?

As a righteous Jew there was only one option open to him. Yet the very word 'divorce' sent a shudder through him. It seemed a terrible price to pay for a situation that appeared to him to be inexplicable. Despite everything, he still loved Mary and was determined to act in a way which afforded her as much protection as could be given. A very discreet and private arrangement was what he proposed. At the end of the day, he had to be seen to do what was right . . .

Joseph certainly had a sensible head on his shoulders and a righteous heart in his ribcage. When, after much agonising consideration, he decided on a quiet divorce, it was the most understandable course of action. Everyone would commend his sensible behaviour, his choice to package matters neatly. Priests would applaud his adherence to the law. Businessmen would endorse his actions as being critical to his future as a carpenter of drive and determination. Flamboyant champions of social etiquette would speak well of his resolve to sever all links with impropriety.

How plausible all this sounds, and how righteous it was, too. The remarkable part of this story is that God's reasoning placed an entirely different meaning on the events taking place. For the only time in history a human egg had been fertilised by the Holy Spirit. Such a sinless conception carried God's favour, not his judgement. It was all part of his plan. In his Gospel, Matthew presents us with two perspectives to the story: on one hand Joseph's viewpoint; on the other, God's purposes. Joseph's decision to divorce came through his human mind, clouded with his own interpretation of the situation. Without God's inspiration, the human mind cannot grasp the plans of God. Our own wisdom, however sensible and constructive, can still miss God's best. In contrast to Joseph's turbulent mind, Matthew calmly records, 'All this took place to fulfil what the Lord had said . . .' It was all in God's plan. Predicted long ago, this incident was no accident. God was in control.

That comforting news was conveyed to Joseph as he slept fitfully one night. The battle of his love and loyalty could be resolved; both could be preserved. There was no need to sacrifice one for the other. God had made sense of the inexplicable.

Joseph's struggle to understand God's mysterious ways has been part of my own experience. When I was dating my wife Honor before we were engaged, our relationship was sometimes hampered by our past emotional baggage. There were times when we struggled to convey our true feelings for one another; we were not in touch with our emotions. Personally, I found it difficult to lighten up and 'be' in the relationship. Things did not always look healthy. Well-meaning friends spoke understandable words of caution to us about the future of our relationship. I am sure I would have done the same if I had been observing a similar situation with other people.

Something in me, however, refused to give up. I remember reading of Joseph's pain, and the angel's words to him so many years ago spoke comfort into my own soul: 'Do not be afraid.' An assurance was conceived in my heart that, despite the difficulties, God was still outworking his purposes. I felt he had promised that out of the deep winter of our relationship, spring would surely come.

That conviction never left me, and, as we prayed our way forward, Honor and I found God gracious and faithful to his word. As springtime came, we were engaged, then married ten months later. Although God had not provided all the answers to our 'Whys?', he had made enough sense of that difficult situation to allow us to go on. And since then we have grown together in love and experienced much joy together in our marriage.

I share this story, not to lay down a blueprint or to predict how God will act with you, but simply to demonstrate how Joseph's lesson from long ago can still teach us today. It was no never-to-be-repeated episode. Our tendency is to erect frameworks of behaviour within which we hope God will act. When circumstances thrust us over these boundaries, we are propelled into the insecurity of the unknown, causing us to question God's activity beyond our previously defined parameters. However, the work of God's Spirit in transforming us at the very deepest level means that we cannot always expect him to follow what in our opinion is a predictable pattern. Against all reason, God may root an assurance within us that what doesn't make sense in our eyes most certainly does in his.

In the face of the inexplicable, discernment is needed to identify God's purposes in the problems. Sometimes we need to ask for the prayers and counsel of trusted friends, but ultimately we need the inner conviction of God to pursue the path he has chosen for us. Joseph did not choose an easy path and he would not have many understanding travelling companions. God's voice was his guide, and with the conviction it brought he took Mary to be his wife. Joseph was learning just how close God could be when times were tough. God was not silent. In fact, he was speaking the very words which Joseph, and we, too, in similar circumstances, desperately need to hear: 'Do not be afraid.'

Prayer

O come, O come, Emmanuel,
and teach me to recognise your purposes
in the inexplicabilities of life,
that the difficult paths I tread
may be part of your perfect plan for me.
Reassure my anxious heart,
as you did for Joseph,
and speak those words of comfort I need to hear:
that nothing is beyond your control,
that I need not be afraid
because you are with me.
Amen.

SPECIAL FRIENDS

Reading: Luke 1:5-25, 39-45

Sustained by Joseph's commitment to her, Mary left Nazareth for the Judean hill country. Not only did Joseph support this time of seclusion for the sake of Mary's privacy, but Mary herself longed for companionship with another woman who would understand the momentous events which had overtaken her. For Mary, the choice of companion was obvious. Elizabeth was then six months into what could only be a supernatural pregnancy. How could Mary not be drawn to this elderly woman, whose womb, like Sarah's from ancient times, had been opened late in life? Elizabeth, too, was experiencing a miracle within her own body.

Mary felt closer to her relative than ever before. She had been bursting to share her news, yet fear of her family's and neighbours' reactions had stifled her. Now she knew she could unstop her feelings. As she hurried to Elizabeth's home, Mary thanked God that the two of them could spend this time together.

In those months Elizabeth came to be a rich source of encouragement to Mary. A mother in the Lord to the mother of the Lord. Mary could not have wished for a more godly older woman who could speak maturity and faith into the young heart of the Lord's handmaiden. Elizabeth was a unique gift at a unique time.

This was a most remarkable conjunction of two women, thrust together by the extraordinary purposes of God. Two women bearing sons; one despite barrenness, the other despite virginity. Two wombs, both occupied by children of promise. Mary and Elizabeth: a pair of maternal miracles.

Mary's entrance into the home of Elizabeth and Zechariah ushered in a profound change in that household. For Mary had not come alone; she brought the very presence of Christ with her, as he grew in the secret place of her womb. Elizabeth took no time in recognising the divine visitor whom Mary had carried over the threshold: 'But why am I so favoured, that the mother of my Lord should come to me?' John the Baptist was equally receptive. His *in utero* somersaults revealed that he was able to recognise Jesus even while both of them were unborn.

And what of Zechariah? What did he make of this visit? For he is the forgotten character in this episode. I wonder what was going on in his mind. Of course, he was mute throughout the entire period Mary spent with them, his silence a punishment for his earlier unbelief in the God who promised to bring the wildly improbable within the bounds of plausibility. Yet, as the months of Elizabeth's pregnancy went by, Zechariah witnessed in wordless wonder the reality of the very thing he previously did not believe.

When Mary came to stay there were two miracles under one roof. As Zechariah observed his own wife progressing towards her due date, and Mary beginning her own journey of pregnancy, he could not fail to accept the miraculous God who had come so close to his own household. And though he could not speak this audibly, I imagine there was a brightening twinkle in his eyes, which disclosed that he now believed. And, awed at the miracle of his own son's birth, when his tongue was finally loosed, his first words declared his recognition of the one who had visited his home for three precious months: 'Praise be to the Lord, the God of Israel, because he has come . . .'

Isn't it wonderful when God draws people closer together because they realise they are fellow travellers treading the same path? Some good friends of ours have recently become much closer to my wife and me through our shared journeys into marriage. There are other friendships I recall, whose origins lie in times when God sovereignly brought us together with synchronous experiences. Such relationships, like good dovetail joints, are secure and long lasting. What is significant is that these relationships are often formed between people with no previous affinity. It is God's work from start to finish.

Such a relationship was forged at a conference my wife and I were attending. We received prayer from an older couple, the husband a church minister. We were initially drawn together by an idea my wife and I were reflecting upon and which seemed at first to link with the current situation of this couple. It soon became clear that God was doing something much deeper between us, and we shared together for a time each day for the rest of the conference.

Several months later, when we visited them for a weekend, this couple asked if they could become 'spiritual parents' to us. We had been longing to have more contact with older people who could take us under their wing to encourage us in our faith, so we readily accepted their invitation with joy. We are still to discover all that God will do through our relationship, but it is clear he is doing something special and we rejoice in this.

We all need special friends, people with whom we can be real and relaxed. God has made us for loving and caring relationships and it is through them that much of our fulfilment comes. Such special relationships need work; they require us to grow in trust and honesty one with another. They may prove costly in terms of time and love, but the rewards can be immense.

Let us pray for more relationships of this kind. Through them we will glimpse more of God's purposes in the lives of others and gain a deeper appreciation of that same God who came close in Jesus and chose to call us his very own friends.

Prayer

O come, O come, Emmanuel,
and teach me to appreciate
the special friends you have given me.
Thank you for the times we spend together,
for the news we share,
for the ways we laugh and the tears we cry.

This Christmas, cause me to wonder
at how close you came in Jesus,
sharing your very self with us in incarnation,
and calling me your friend.
Amen.

4 DECEMBER

THE MAGNIFICAT

Reading: Luke 1:46-55

Elizabeth's words to Mary about her being blessed through her belief became a trigger releasing a flood of praise from the young girl. The lips which had spoken in submission to the will of divine purpose, now extolled the God behind that great plan. The words rippled over one another, a clear, fresh stream of rich vocabulary.

Elizabeth sat in wonder; the verbal beauty of Mary's words moved her deeply. When Mary had spoken, the two women remained in silence for a time. Two very different generations, the old and the young, sharing miracles within their bodies and vibrant faith through their words. I wonder how those moving lyrics came to be recorded for us. Perhaps Elizabeth was so struck by them that she had Zechariah record them on a scroll, and in years to come would ask her husband to read them to her. Each time those words filled their home, I can imagine them marvelling at all God had done.

And in later years, perhaps that scroll was passed to Mary, who always treasured it. It would have represented for her all she truly felt deep within about her role as the mother of Jesus. That scroll would always have remained a very private memento, until the day, that is, when the doctor, Luke, came to talk with her when he was writing his biography of Jesus. When she recalled those first months of her pregnancy, she could not fail to speak of those words which came out of her deepest being. And maybe it was then that the scroll was brought out of its concealment and Luke asked if he might borrow it for the opening chapter of his narrative . . .

Little did Mary know at that time how significant the words of her Magnificat would become, repeated down the centuries and set to some of the most beautiful music ever composed. There in Zechariah's and Elizabeth's home, she was simply expressing her discoveries of the ways in which she knew God had drawn close to her.

Mary's praise issued initially through her realisation of the mindfulness of God towards her. And this was more wondrous for Mary when she considered her own position before him. In her own words, she viewed herself as one in a 'humble state' (verse 48). In the original Greek this phrase is much more than a statement of Mary's humility, conveying a much stronger impression of humiliation. It implies how unworthy Mary considered herself to be the mother of Jesus. Yet God smiled upon her, despite her own feelings. God was showing Mary special favour at that time. This most favoured of women had begun to realise that God can work mightily even when humiliation is present. Many years later she would learn this most powerfully as recognition came that her own feelings of degradation in bringing about Jesus' birth were only a foreshadowing of his ignominious death, by which God would complete his most telling act.

Mary felt uplifted by God; it was as though he had invited her to a banquet whose table positively groaned under the weight of good things to be enjoyed. It was the humble who were welcome to this feast. All those of proud heart would not find a place at the table.

Mary's joy also sprang from God's faithfulness, not only to

her personally, but also to his people Israel. God had remembered his people and his own word to their ancestors. His promises still stood from generations past. Mary found herself caught up in this great movement of God towards all the peoples of the world.

The enduring words of the Magnificat still resound in churches around the globe. They have become a perpetual personal testimony of a great God performing a great work in an ordinary person.

And that, for me, is the key to this wonderful song. It is not about the great and the famous. It is not concerned with the influential or the powerful. It is the story of a self-effacing teenager who allowed Almighty God to do something special in her life. I like that kind of story, simply because I can relate to it. Personally I'm so glad Mary allowed her story to be told. We know how she treasured many things and pondered them alone. There are many thoughts and memories of those days which will remain forever hers. But what we know is glorious enough to make it the subject of our own reflections.

Many of us are far too shy to admit that anything God has done in our lives is worthy of mention. In contrast to Mary's lips, which spoke forth the goodness of God, those of many believers can be strangely silent. Perhaps this is because we feel that we can only speak of God if it is done in eloquent fashion like it was for Mary. Please allow me now to lay that particular fallacy to rest. Nobody has to give testimony in quite the way Mary did. More often than not we struggle to convey our feelings about what God does for us. The hand of God touches us at levels of our being so profound as to be unseen save by the eye of our Creator. Who is it, then, who claims expertise in speaking of such things? Human language itself is insufficient in riches for such a task.

Instead we should learn increasingly to share as much as we are able, in words which are truly our own, about what God is doing in our lives. It makes for encouragement of others on the journey. Believe it or not, we all have a Magnificat hidden within us – our own story of how an exceptional God is changing us –

and when the time is right, that song will come forth too, another verse to that great song of God's mercy which 'extends to those who fear him, from generation to generation'.

Prayer

O come, O come, Emmanuel,
and let me sing my own Magnificat this Christmas,
a song of thankfulness which truly wells up
as my heartfelt response to your greatness and faithfulness.
Help us to realise it is not eloquence you seek, but honesty,
spoken in words which are truly our own
and with a faith we wish everyone would share.
Amen.

5 DECEMBER

GOD OF THE ORDINARY

Reading: Psalm 139:1-24

Following the drama of the opening weeks of Mary's pregnancy, life had begun to fall into some predictable routines for both of the expectant parents. Joseph had found himself in a very demanding period of work. His carpentry shop positively pulsated with activity all day. Old Joab from the other side of the village had been his usual difficult self – changing his mind several times regarding the style of table leg he really wanted, and wasting no end of precious time which Joseph could ill afford to squander. With Mary not around, Joseph had simply thrown himself headlong into his work. He had always had a strong business sense – had inherited it from his father – and this was just the kind of situation where all his professional acumen needed to be exercised. Of course, he thought often of Mary, and missed her, but his bread-winning instinct drove him into a disciplined routine of work, eat, sleep.

Mary had experienced a return to a quieter existence at Zechariah's and Elizabeth's after the eventful happenings which surrounded the start of her visit to them. She would spend much of her day sitting and sewing, talking endlessly with Elizabeth. She would enjoy walks in the countryside and assisted Elizabeth with domestic chores. Following the excitement of earlier days, her new routine was in some ways a relief and a return to normality.

It was one day, while preparing the main evening meal, that Mary remembered particularly the presence of Jesus within her. It was a strange moment, hardly definable in words, yet thoroughly authentic. There she stood, spoon in hand, stirring the pot of stew over the fire. The zenith of normality. There was no one else around. Just her . . . and Jesus. This simple revelation startled her. She could not feel him; she could not see him. And yet he was there. Suddenly the preparation of that meal was transformed. It had become a shared activity, a simple development of the rela-tionship between mother and child. Through a foetus in Mary's womb, God had penetrated the veil of the familiar and shown this expectant mother that she could expect him to be close even at those most ordinary times.

Familiarity is the fog which so often obscures our ability to perceive God's closeness; routine can blur a beautifully sharp awareness of him. Today's reading comes to dissipate that fog and focus that blurred image. In this Psalm David catalogues the dealings of a God who meets with him at every twist and turn of normal life. Its lyrics are well known and that in itself may be a barrier to us experiencing its full impact. So perhaps you will allow me to reword some of them now, to help us more fully appreciate our inescapable God:

O Lord, you have looked me over, rifled through my life's contents and got to the bottom of every issue that currently resides there. You know when I've flopped in that chair at the end of the day, weary and drained like a deflated balloon, out of puff and out of patience. You see me in the morning, when my hair resembles a child's first attempt at knitting, and I can't face my own face in the mirror. You observe me as I close the front door behind me, dreading what lies before me in the day, and wanting to be home the moment I've left. You see me when I come back through that same door, my confidence at rock bottom because of a failure that day which stripped me of all my self-worth. You hear the words I speak each day, and the ones in my head that I really mean, but never vocalise. Where can I flee from your presence? If I go up to the top deck of the Number 42 bus, you are there; if I go down to the basement of my local department store, you are there. The darkness can't fool you for light is part of the very nature of your presence. O Lord, you know all about me and are always with me.

I am learning to open my eyes and ears much more as I go about my daily life. The drudgery of our routine existence does not have to become our enemy when it comes to appreciating God's presence. 300 years ago a French monk by the name of Brother Lawrence spent much of his day preparing food in his monastery kitchen. Despite this humble existence, characterised by endless routine, he developed in the depths of his soul a quiet contemplation of the reality of God's presence. Brother Lawrence called this awareness 'the practice of the presence of God'. God's presence became as much a part of his life in the kitchen as it was in the chapel, whether he was on his feet chopping carrots, or on his knees petitioning the Almighty.

Brother Lawrence never claimed to have a great secret which was his alone. He simply championed the cause of God in the commonplace of life. In fact, Brother Lawrence would probably have rebuffed any dichotomy between the common and the sacred. He is our encouragement to do the same. We are not saying that life does not have its routines. We are claiming that these very routines can be impregnated by God's presence and therefore can even be an offering to him. In this way, even the dullest duties for Brother Lawrence – and ourselves – can be viewed as being of interest to God.

The trouble with us is that we probably have a lifetime of routines which have deserved, in our opinion, no higher status than that of drudgery. We are not being asked to pretend that a task we find tedious is not. The example of Mary, of David and of Brother Lawrence, teaches us to see God even in that situation. We can therefore seek his help and strength when routine and chores threaten to drive us round the bend.

In a society where the limelight of the sensational is so often sought, the commonplace has become relegated backstage. Let us examine again how we view the ordinariness of our lives, and recognise that this shadowy and disregarded domain is just as much God's as our high days and holidays, and he is ready to meet us here too.

Prayer

O come, O come, Emmanuel,
and teach me to be ready to see you
in the commonplace of life.
You are not remote from my routines,
nor distant from my dullest duties.
Help me to witness your pervasion of the very ordinary,
that together with you I can face the humdrum of my life,
knowing that you are there
to give me the strength each day to go on.
Amen.

6 DECEMBER

IN A TIME OF DOUBT

Reading: Matthew 28:16-20

With Mary away from Nazareth, life had not been easy for Joseph. He had been able to deflect the villagers' questions about Mary's absence by explaining that she had 'just gone to visit Elizabeth'. Further probing was appeased by this answer, much to Joseph's relief.

It was not the scrutiny of his neighbours which troubled him most; instead it was the instability of his own convictions. Not that he was experiencing a major crisis of faith over all that was happening. He was simply struggling to embrace the reality of it, particularly when Mary was not around. Somehow her physical presence reassured him of God's purposes, for her own body played host to a heavenly gift.

But now, alone in his workshop on a humdrum kind of day, he felt bereft, not only of Mary's company, but God's also. Why, at this time, did he feel the need for some physical reminder of God's reality? Weren't his recent encounters with angels enough? Joseph felt sheepish at best and guilty at worst for his lack of conviction. It wasn't the kind of thing he wanted to talk about. And frankly in Nazareth, with Mary away, there was no one he felt he could talk to. The villagers would have to know at some stage about the pregnancy, but Joseph was in no hurry to inform them at present. Since the reality of the situation was temporarily lost on him, he knew he couldn't provide adequate explanations for it to anyone else.

It wasn't until Mary returned and shared with Joseph her 'ordinary day' experience that he began to view matters differently. Mary and Joseph were both learning that God's interventions do not have to be visible to be valid.

The human race has renewed its quest for the secret of faith in an invisible God in each successive generation. Whether it is expressed or not, doubt in God's presence because of his invisibility is commonplace. At heart we are creatures who believe that what is real must be rational. And a God who claims to be present, but who cannot be seen, challenges our logic. A hide-and-seek God appears to drive a hard bargain when he calls us to believe he is really there. Yet this is the key to faith: 'But hope that is seen is no hope at all. Who hopes for what he already has?' (Romans 8:24). By challenging our reasoning, God stretches us to place our faith in him.

Thomas is surely the most famous biblical character who struggled with doubt over issues of faith and sight. Thomas' words on the evening of the first Easter day succinctly summarise how many of us would view the question of faith: 'Unless I see . . . I will not believe' (John 20:25). Jesus did not withdraw from Thomas, even though he doubted. The risen Christ drew near again to show his doubting disciple the full extent of his love for him and to encourage him to believe, even without seeing him. 'Blessed are those who have not seen and yet have believed' (John 20:29). Jesus invited Thomas to test the reality of his presence. He did not shy away from a thorough investigation. He was prepared to bear close scrutiny.

During that formative post-Easter period, Jesus included even those followers who doubted. Take that incident in our reading for today, when he gave his disciples the Great Commission, encouraging them with those unfading words: 'And surely I am with you always to the very end of the age' (Matthew 28:20). Was this promise given to a group who were free from reservations? Not when we read there were some who doubted (verse 17). Jesus' promise of his presence is made to those who doubt as well as those who don't. The deeper we trust him, the closer we will enjoy relationship with him. But his presence is not withheld through doubt. He is still there, longing to draw us from the cocoon of doubt, to fly as a butterfly on wings of faith.

I am trained as a mathematician. In this subject I deal with absolutes which are visible and proven. $2 + 2 = 4$, QED. In mathematics ambiguities are completely alien. Rigidity of proof leaves no room whatsoever for doubt. It would be utterly inconceivable for a mathematician to make a statement like, 'Now, I'd just like you to believe, on trust you understand, that $x = 4$.' To introduce even the slightest notion of faith into mathematics would cause the entire system to collapse instantly.

Maybe you are not a mathematician (and I can hear many of you rejoicing over this fact!). But even if you are not, I trust you will sympathise with me when it comes to issues of faith. I would hazard a guess that even those of you who are not logical thinkers still have your struggles with this issue of believing in a God who cannot be seen. It goes against everything we consider rational.

I have needed to learn down the years that faith in God is not like proof in mathematics. To believe in a God who is close but unseen is not a matter for intellectual acrobatics. It is a question of relationship, not rationale. My relationship with God authenticates his presence. The great preacher Dr Billy Graham was once asked how we knew that God existed. 'He must be there,' came the reply, 'because I spoke with him this morning.'

Mathematics is proof enough of the incredibly detailed order which God built into our world. But God never intended us to relate to him with mathematical minds. Let's all breathe a sigh of relief about this. Instead let us commit ourselves afresh this Christmas to pursue that most precious of relationships with God, through which we will truly see him. Jesus came to earth, not to appeal to our reason but to our hearts, those vessels of love he beckons us to pour out as an offering to him.

Prayer

O come, O come, Emmanuel,
and draw me deeper into relationship with you.
Thank you that you do not withdraw your presence from me

when I doubt.
Help me to believe that your hands are gentle enough
to hold my often fragile faith,
that you take more notice of the trust you do see
than my lack of it.
This Christmas, help me to see you came
for the sake of relationship, not rationale.
Amen.

7 DECEMBER

FAMILY LIKENESS?

Reading: Mark 6:1-6a

'I wonder what he'll look like, Joseph,' asked Mary one day.

'Yes, I've been wondering that myself,' he replied. It was not such a straightforward question to answer. For theirs was no usual pregnancy and no copybook child.

Conversations between prospective parents about their forthcoming child's physical attributes were commonplace among the villagers of Nazareth. There were the usual fears like, 'I hope he won't have your bandy legs', as well as the hopeful expectations like, 'She'll do well if she has your beauty and my brains.'

Mary and Joseph knew that they could not quite enter into this discussion, although the question still intrigued them. Joseph felt more detached, for he knew that genetically he had played no part in Jesus' conception. He could not expect Jesus to inherit any of his physical characteristics. Mary, on the other hand, was fascinated with the extent to which Jesus might bear her own family's likeness. Would she, in his face, catch a glimpse of her own? Family traits and heavenly glory in the contours of human skin?

And it wasn't just a matter of physical likeness. What about Jesus' character? What could they expect him to be like? Would he be irritable when tired and hungry like any other toddler? Would God's Son be subject to the 'terrible twos'? As he grew up, would he test the boundaries like any normal developing child? That was the issue – would he be 'normal'? Mary and Joseph didn't really know how to answer that question. How can you predict the personality of God's Son? One thing they did know: some surprises were in store. They felt quite daunted at the prospect of parenting Jesus, as they couldn't properly prepare. Who else has parented a child like Jesus? They were treading their own path.

And yet an incredible thrill would shimmer through them as they considered their guardian roles. Daunted at the prospect, yet awed at the privilege of being the first people on earth to look into the face of God's own Son.

The children of some good friends of mine delightfully model the inheritance of family likeness. The husband bears a tiny sinus (small hole) in his skin behind his right ear. All three of his daughters carry the same mark. I remember the joy with which he showed me the mark, replicated in miniature behind his youngest daughter's ear, when she was but weeks old.

We do not know if Jesus bore any physical likeness to either Mary or Joseph. If we are true to the prophecy of scripture, we would not be wrong to claim that the way Jesus looked was not remarkable. In Isaiah's words, 'He had no beauty or majesty to attract us to him, nothing in his appearance that we should desire him' (Isaiah 53:2b). On a physical level, we would not have singled him out as special. If we had not seen him before, he would not stand out to us in an identity parade.

It was in expectations of his character rather than his looks that discrepancies arose. Jesus simply didn't turn out as people thought he would. At times he became a disappointment even to his own human guardians. There was that time when, at the age of 12, Jesus stayed behind at the temple in Jerusalem, much to the consternation of his parents. 'Didn't you know I had to be in my Father's house?' (Luke 2:49) was his seemingly nonchalant response to their reprimand. During his public ministry, Jesus was also accused of madness by his family (Mark 3:21). The Palestinian public at large struggled to square their expectations of a holy man with the actions of Jesus. Physical contact with lepers, close association with prostitutes, visits to 'sinners' and healings on the Sabbath were not, in their opinion, fitting for a prophet. I can imagine some people saying to Jesus, 'You really shouldn't be seen here doing this. I mean, it won't do your reputation any good.' Such comments would have betrayed a lack of understanding of Jesus' mission. It was not about reputation, but relinquishment. As St Paul wrote, Jesus 'made himself nothing, taking the very nature of a servant' (Philippians 2:7). He had come to give up even his own life, all for the sake of love.

Perhaps the group who became most at odds with Jesus' conduct were the inhabitants of his home town. The villagers of Nazareth simply could not believe that the carpenter's son they thought they knew so well could be anyone other than just that. They were well acquainted with his family and were not about to impute any remarkable qualities to them. Why should Jesus be any different? In their own words, 'What's this wisdom that has been given him, that he even does miracles? Isn't this the carpenter? Isn't this Mary's son?' (Mark 6:2-3). In other words, a worker of wood could not be a worker of wonders.

How wrong they were. And how wrong we can be, too. That old maxim, 'Familiarity breeds contempt' holds no less true today. When we think we know Jesus, we must be careful we do not underestimate his uniqueness. True closeness to Christ brings uncomfortable truths about how little we actually do know him. Our pride can play a powerful part in breeding wrong expectations about Jesus. The inhabitants of Nazareth found it hard to admit that they had misjudged the man they thought they knew. They also believed that physical heritage is the only determinant of future character. They knew his parents and siblings, so Jesus could be categorised in the family mould. After all, they would reason, like father, like son. The irony was that this reasoning would have led them to welcome Jesus, if only they had grasped that the Father he spoke of was his heavenly one. He had a special heritage which made all the difference.

Amongst the clamour of disapproval which so often encompassed him, Jesus was able to hear the one voice which really mattered, that of his own Father. And whenever he heard that voice, it spoke of his pleasure towards the Son who had submitted to his Father's will. We also who have yielded to the Lordship of Christ have entered into our own inheritance and can receive that same approval from our Father. And as we experience more of that closeness of relationship, we will find ourselves growing into a new family likeness, reflecting the Lord's glory in our own lives, until the day it will come to completion in heaven. 'And just as we have borne the likeness of the earthly man, so shall we bear the likeness of the man from heaven' (1 Corinthians 15:49). Mary and Joseph first caught a glimpse of that glory veiled in humanity in the blood-tinged face of their first-born on the night he was born. This Christmas let us take a fresh look at Jesus and ask, by the work of his Spirit within us, to become more like him.

Prayer

O come, O come, Emmanuel,
and pierce the cloud of familiarity
which threatens to blur the true picture of who you are.
Help me to see you afresh this Christmas,
not with the tired eyes of annual routine,
but with eyes of excited discovery,
that as I gaze with face unveiled,
I may bear more strongly the family likeness of your people.
Amen.

8 DECEMBER

EQUAL TO THE TASK?

Reading: 1 Corinthians 1:26-29

Now at the end of her first trimester of pregnancy, Mary was becoming all too aware of the responsibility laid upon her as the mother of God's Son. Her time with Elizabeth had played a significant role in those early months since the day Gabriel's words changed her life completely. But now Elizabeth was nearly due herself and Mary felt it time to return to Nazareth. In recent weeks she had begun to notice other mothers with children in her neighbourhood. She observed the tireless affection these women gave their offspring: tender care and loving rebukes. She witnessed their total commitment, despite frustration and exhaustion. 'Oh, Lord,' she prayed, 'I don't think I have it in me to be a good mother.'

She felt like a child, thrust into the threatening world of adulthood well before her time. But there was no turning back; Gabriel's words had closed the door of childhood for ever. Now she stood on the other side, unsure of herself, and painfully aware of her inadequacies. She wished this didn't have to be her first pregnancy, not with Jesus. She'd listened to many mothers who told her how they were much more relaxed during subsequent pregnancies. What was God up to, giving his Son a nervous, first-time mother? For something so important as this, surely a novice was not a wise choice?

Mary sighed. She knew she was carrying not just Jesus but all the responsibility that motherhood entailed. 'Oh, Lord,' she prayed again, 'have I really got it in me to do this?'

Mary's feelings of inadequacy would have been entirely understandable. She felt young and vulnerable, facing a unique task for which she was unprepared. Here again in the Christmas story we witness a God who turned the tables on how we would expect him to act.

Human reason persuades us to grant responsibility only to those we deem qualified to handle it. We look for previous experience, certificates of skill, references of merit. Yet for the birth of his Son, necessity demanded a different approach. For an immaculate conception required a virgin, and a virgin mother would have to be a first-time mother. Jesus' route to earth came through inexperience.

Christmas represents only one way in which God worked in this way. It's in his nature to define what is wise and what is foolish. 'But God chose the foolish things of the world to shame the wise; God chose the weak things of the world to shame the strong. He chose the lowly things of this world and the despised things – and the things that are not – to nullify the things that are' (1 Corinthians 1:27-28). God chooses inexperience to neutralise self-pride.

Mary does not stand alone in scripture with her feelings of inadequacy. The Bible is a catalogue of unlikely novices whom God transformed. Noah was a farmer who turned his hand to shipbuilding and saved his family and the fauna of the earth. Moses was a shepherd with a criminal record who had never given a public address, yet became one of Israel's greatest leaders. David was a shepherd and the youngest of his family, yet God chose his veins to carry royal blood. Isaiah lamented his own sinfulness among a people of the same, but received the mercy of God and the mission of a prophet.

Two other beginners deserve mention. Charged with assuming the mantle of Israel's judge, Gideon confesses that he is the least of the least. Notice God's reply: 'I will be with you' (Judges 6:16). Jeremiah's opinion of himself was not affirming either: 'I am only a child.' God's response? 'I am with you' (Jeremiah 1:8). Inexperience becomes unimportant when an expert God is close by. First-timers need not fear when the true God of all time is at hand.

As I write these words, my life is in a state of flux as I make a change in employment. Faced with an open choice, I have needed to look to God and to his work deep within me to sense the next step. At times I have doubted my own abilities and considered myself some kind of employment misfit. I have studied my CV and thought, 'Is this all I am worth? Is this the measure of the real me?' Such doubts have only been intensified by rejections from my applications, particularly when I thought I was suited and qualified for the position. Friends have sought to encourage me at this time, but I have often felt out of my depth, treading water only on the basis of qualities others say I possess. Feelings of insignificance have been more prevalent now than at any other time in my life. I have come as close as I ever could to understanding how some people can feel they are just a faint watermark on the pages of history.

I have needed to take a hard look at myself and a hard look at God. Part of my own encouragement has come from taking a fresh look at the Christmas story. For there I see a God who is not only the final arbiter of our worth, but the faithful companion in our meagreness. Part of our fear of the unknown comes from the anticipation that we might face it alone. But footsteps into the unfamiliar become less unnerving when we have a companion.

That old chestnut, 'There's a first time for everything' has never given me much help when I've undertaken a new challenge. Better by far is the knowledge of God's presence as I go out on a limb. When Jesus called his first followers into a new way of life, it was not to send them into isolation. I am struck that first and foremost, his invitation was simply to be with him (Mark 3.14). His call was not via entrance examinations, but by a word of welcome into companionship. The same was true for Mary, who, even during her nine months of pregnancy, was beginning to enjoy that close-ness with Jesus whom she had welcomed into her life. And the same is true for us, too.

We may say, 'I don't think I have it in me.' But with God's Spirit resident in our lives, we have all the resources we could ever need within us. God declares we are of age, even when we feel like a little child who has never grown up. We may cry, 'I can't', but God draws near to whisper, 'You can with me.'

Prayer

O come, O come, Emmanuel,
and teach me that my inadequacies
need not paralyse me.
Draw close to me this Christmas
and show me how your grace is sufficient
for all my meagreness,
how your strength is perfected in weakness.
May your hand grip tightly my own
when it trembles at what the future holds.
Thank you that you walk with me into the unknown.
Amen.

TAKING THINGS FURTHER

Summary

The events occurring in the early months of Mary's pregnancy are amongst the most startling recorded in all scripture. Here was the fulfilment of long years of prophecy. Mary's womb became the sanctuary for God's silent invasion of the world. As heaven watched with bated breath, the Holy Spirit skilfully presided over a perfect conception. Humanity and divinity mingled in a human cell, which then divided. An embryo gradually formed; the Messiah had come.

For Mary, of course, these events changed her life for ever. She came to welcome this secret life of Christ within her, and with the help of special friends like Elizabeth, truly treasured all that God was doing. Those early days of Mary's pregnancy teach us about allowing the presence of Christ into our lives for him to work in us and through us. We are challenged to ask ourselves how welcome the Lord really is in our lives. But for Mary there were also times of doubt and feelings of inadequacy that every first expectant mother knows. Mary found strength through God's promises to her. Reflecting upon her example can help us to learn ways of reaching out to God in our times of uncertainty.

The events surrounding the Annunciation were wildly beyond anything Joseph had in mind. He experienced a tortuous dilemma in the days following Gabriel's announcement of Mary's conception. The early days of Mary's pregnancy encourage us to bring before God the circumstances which seem to us to be without rhyme or reason. Advent is a time for us, like Mary and Joseph, to learn more about trusting God's word and finding faith to face the future.

Discussion questions

1. What does it mean to welcome the Lord into our lives? How can we deny him access? How does the way in which Mary received Gabriel's news of Annunciation help us to open our lives to the Lord?

2. When life doesn't make sense, how can this affect the way we view God? What lessons can we learn from the way Joseph handled the news of Mary's pregnancy that will help us see God's purposes?

3. Consider some Christians you know of who inspire you in your faith. They may be close friends or people you know about through other sources. What is it about them that encourages you? How could you deepen your relationships with other Christians, so as to be more aware of God at work among you?

4. If you are in a group, allow each member to share one thing they have learned in their faith over the last month. Savour each other's stories. In prayer, give thanks to God for his goodness and ask him for opportunities to make his love known to others. If you are on your own, recall one recent encouragement in your faith and write your own version of the Magnificat to express your praise to God.

5. Think of creative ways in which you could use some of the ordinary routines in your life to remember how close the Lord is.

6. In what ways have you doubted God? What helped you at those times? What encouragements can you find in the Christmas story to help you?

7. What characterises an individual who is full of the Lord's presence? What characterises a Church which enjoys a strong sense of the Lord's presence?

8. Make a list of as many attributes of God's goodness as you can. How do these qualities help us in the situations we face (e.g. the dependability of God can help us when we feel insecure)?

SECOND TRIMESTER
9-16 DECEMBER

9 DECEMBER

LOOKING AFTER GOD

Reading: Matthew 25:31-46

Joseph paused at his work; his saw lay snug in its newly cut groove. The carpenter was deep in thought once more. It was good to have Mary back from her stay with Zechariah and Elizabeth. Their son had now been born and news of the birth had reached Nazareth swiftly, causing no end of excited conversations as to the future of this exceptional child: 'What then is this child going to be?' All this and Mary's presence close by again only served to underline that, in less than half a year, he too would be holding a baby boy. He did not want to play down the significance of Zechariah's and Elizabeth's son, but he knew that the child he would hold would be more special still.

No matter how hard he tried, he could not feel relaxed about the idea of parenting. It was not so much the actual task itself, but rather the thought of parenting Jesus. Lately Joseph had become rather over-protective of Mary, seeking to cushion her from anything which, in his opinion, might remotely harm the baby. Mary was much more relaxed. 'He's quite safe, Joseph,' she would say softly. But for Joseph, the pregnancy was the easy stage. True, Jesus was safe at present, fully nourished and protected within Mary. But Joseph had become concerned for what would happen after the birth. All kind of fears raced around his head, mercilessly taunting him. 'I might drop him or hold him the wrong way.' In his worst moments, Joseph wasn't even sure that he would have the courage to touch the baby, let alone pick him up. Could he, really, bring himself to touch the skin of God's own Son?

'Lord, you're asking me to look after you, but I need you to look after me. After all, isn't that what your job is? You're not supposed to give us the job of looking after you – are you?'

Mary and Joseph had a unique task as the human guardians of the infant Christ. Joseph may well have been worried that this should be his job; he considered that God was reversing the roles of responsibility. But God was not abdicating his duty; he would still be looking after the couple, even as they ministered to him in the newborn Christ.

We may be tempted to feel that such a unique task is far removed from our own lives. But we would be wrong to make this assumption. Although Jesus has physically left the earth, the opportunities remain to minister to him and realise he is near.

Papa Panov is the old shoemaker in the delightful children's Christmas tale by Ruben Saillens. It's Christmas Eve and Papa Panov sits alone in his shop; his memories are his only companions. He reads the Christmas story, wishing that Jesus could come to his shop so that he could give him a gift. Papa Panov falls asleep and in his dreams hears the voice of Jesus: 'Papa Panov, you wished that I would come to your shop. Look into the street tomorrow and I will surely come. Be sure you recognise me, for I shall not say who I am.'

All next day the old shoemaker waits excitedly by the window of his shop, wondering how he will recognise the Son of God. Various people come by: an old roadsweeper to whom he gives a cup of coffee, a poor young woman with a baby to whom he gives a tiny pair of shoes he has made. As dusk begins to fall, he wonders if Jesus will ever come. The street is soon deserted and Papa Panov sadly closes up his shop and sits back in his old chair. 'It was only a dream,' he muses, 'but I so wanted him to come.'

Suddenly it is as if someone else is in the room. Through the watery veil of his tears, Papa Panov sees a long line of people – all those he had met that day. 'Didn't you see me?' came the whisper of the same voice he had heard the night before.

'Who are you?' cries Papa Panov.

'I was hungry and you gave me food, thirsty and you gave me water, I was cold and you took me in. All these people you have helped today – when you helped them, you were helping me!' And then all is quiet.

Papa Panov sits for a while, a sparkle in his eyes appearing through his evaporating tears. 'So he came after all.'

The parallel between Jesus' words in this story and his own in the parable of the sheep and goats is obvious. This parable is both striking and shocking. Striking, in that we can minister to and encounter Christ in others; shocking, in that a lack of care for others is a withdrawal of love from him.

I know that in times past I have taken this parable too lightly. In so doing I have passed by the Christ whose own piercing eyes have looked to me through those of people I so casually disregarded. Rather than avoiding his gaze, I am learning to meet it head on in the eyes of those who look to me for care. I do not always know how to help; I am sometimes too paralysed by my own fear to give of myself.

God is indeed close, ready to meet us in the humanity around us, however broken that may seem. St Teresa of Avila once wrote, 'Though we do not have our Lord with us in bodily presence, we have our neighbour, who for the ends of love and loving service, is as good as our Lord himself.' This is our encouragement to reach beyond ourselves – that at the end of our outstretched arm of love, we will touch the Lord, who has chosen to reveal himself in those around us. And Jesus in his parable tells us that a greater reward awaits those who live for others: a homecoming into a kingdom whose value outweighs anything we could ever give away in this life. And the Saviour, whose gaze we meet cloaked in human need, will bid us welcome into the realm where his presence will never be hidden.

Prayer

O come, O come, Emmanuel,
reveal yourself through those I meet.
Allow me to recognise your eyes in theirs,
to realise that a simple act of service that touches their heart

blesses yours also.
Draw me from self-interest to reach into the pain of others
with your perfect love which binds up the broken-hearted
and brings Good News to the poor.
Amen.

10 DECEMBER

FAMILY TREES

Reading: Matthew 1:1-17

Joseph was intensely proud of his ancestry, his descent from his hero King David. As a boy he loved to hear his own father Jacob's rendering of those swashbuckling tales of gallantry as David subdued his enemies. How could he forget that day when, on his tenth birthday, he made his own sling and bombarded the old fig tree on the edge of the village as if it were Goliath? To be of David's line was a privilege indeed.

Although Joseph could not fully grasp it, he knew that Jesus' birth into this family line was of special significance. What was it that Gabriel had said to Mary about Jesus? 'The Lord God will give him the throne of his father David, and he will reign over the house of Jacob for ever.' This was heady stuff. Was Jesus to be a new King David? Was he destined to sweep aside the Roman invaders and restore the kingdom to Israel? Joseph checked himself. Surely this was madness; all this was far too grand a future. Everyone knew that nothing good ever came out of Nazareth. Joseph had wondered about Jesus being God's chosen Messiah, but was confused. He knew enough from the scriptures to know that the Messiah would come from Bethlehem and Joseph had no intention of moving there . . .

Despite the glories of his royal ancestor, Joseph was painfully aware of the dishonour which some members had conferred on his family line. He could not deny what had taken place, but he tried not to dwell unnecessarily on these unsavoury episodes in Israel's history.

Until Gabriel's appearance to Mary and his own dealings with angels, Joseph had feared that, because of Israel's unfaithfulness, God had again abandoned his people. The oppressive rule of the Romans certainly did not encourage the Israelites to feel that God was close, and yet, even though the full picture was unclear, something stirred in Joseph that perhaps God was on the move again.

Recently my father has been delving into our family tree. Concentrating mainly on my mother's side, he has successfully traced the line back into the 1800s, but has encountered difficulties going further back because of the need to identify correctly two people with the same name. His search has seen him poring over parish records, scouring graveyards for tombstones and unlocking the treasures in the mind of a nonagenarian aunt of my mother. By so doing, he has recaptured some of our family's forgotten past.

Of course, overturning the stones of time involves the risk of allowing the present daylight to fall upon unpleasant truths which hitherto have long remained buried. The Israelites were not spared the records of their past. Jesus' line of heritage is as great a miscellany of humanity as we could expect to find. Within his family tree, great boughs of heroism flourish side by side with offshoots of terrible evil. Branches of admirable godliness intertwine with those of deplorable unfaithfulness. This tree has a chequered history indeed.

Maybe it would be best not to look too closely at some of the branches. After all, there are plenty of presentable sections to enjoy. But there is an important point to be made by recognising the rotten limbs of this most famous family tree, as well as those that are healthy.

This tree is rooted in the God of history. His Spirit has been there in every generation. Like the sap rising and coursing through a tree's branches, so God has provided life for each person to receive. Some have chosen to reject that life and, like branches from whom the sap is cut off, they have rotted. But the death of one part does not deny new life elsewhere. A survey of Jesus' genealogy reveals where healthy growth has emerged after a period of corruption. God is a long-term God, at work in every generation.

If eternity were a forest, it would be easy to feel lost in our own family tree – an insignificant twig out on a limb. This is compounded if we recoil at the thought of the branches from the past which gave us life. Our family background may not have been positive; we may be first-generation Christian, with no spiritual heritage from which to draw support.

Jesus provided his own horticultural analogy to help us know that we can be close to him. 'I am the vine; you are the branches. If a man remains in me, and I in him, he will bear much fruit; apart from me you can do nothing. If anyone does not remain in me, he is like a branch that is thrown away and withers' (John 15:5-6). The important place to be grafted in life is not so much into our family tree, but into the true Vine, Jesus. The stability of this Vine stands in stark contrast to the insecurity we can feel within our own family circle.

Whenever we feel lost and insignificant, a cry for remembrance comes from our heart. The pages of scripture detail the actions of a God who has never forgotten those who call to him in this way. If the most famous cry for remembrance in the Bible is anything to go by, we can be confident that whatever our background or current circumstances, we can expect to enjoy the closeness of relationship that comes from being grafted into God's life-giving Vine.

That famous cry for remembrance came gasping from the lips of the penitent thief who hung beside Jesus that first Good Friday. The background and upbringing of that man may have been stacked against him. His own actions had certainly brought shame to his own family tree. But there was another tree that day – the cross of Christ – from which that thief would receive words of precious mercy to change his inheritance for ever: 'Today you will be with me in Paradise.'

Prayer

O come, O come, Emmanuel,
Root of Jesse, promised for many generations.
Let me be grafted into you,
the life-giving Vine,
drawing all my strength and resources from you.
Thank you that as I grow in my relationship with you,
I may leave behind for ever in eternity's forest
the boughs of my family's tree
which are best forgotten.
Grant me courage when the stones of time are overturned,
knowing that, though some discoveries are unwelcome,
you have already surveyed them in their darkness;
you paid their price
and beckon me still to Paradise with you.
Amen.

11 DECEMBER

NO CORNER-CUTTING GOD

Reading: Hebrews 4:14–5:10

Lately in Nazareth, long after the working day was over, sounds of activity in the carpentry shop could still be heard. Joseph planed the edge of the wood in his vice, the shavings twirling in a brief frolic with the air before settling on the workshop floor. He ran his finger along the wood, so smooth now in contrast to the coarseness of his own hands. Removing the contents of the vice, he turned to a second workbench, where he nailed the new piece in place. Taking his chisel and mallet, he painstakingly etched his initials in the corner of the headboard; all his work was identified in this way. In the flickering light of his lamp, he stood back to survey his craftsmanship.

Yes, it was a fine crib, to be sure. Personally designed by Joseph, there could be, in his opinion, nowhere better to lay the Son of God after he'd been born. Joseph had begun to think of that special moment when, as a family, they would all be together in their own home. He touched the crib, rocking it gently on the workbench. Proud of his work, he knew he could only give the best for Jesus . . .

Five months later Joseph stood in the Bethlehem stable and stared long and hard at the stone feeding trough. Under the circumstances it was the best he could find for a crib. He'd scrubbed it out as best he could and packed it with clean straw. Mary sat quietly nearby, nursing the newborn babe. A tinge of sadness rested upon Joseph, nestling uneasily with the great joy he'd experienced at Jesus' birth. He sighed deeply as Mary laid the now-sleeping infant into the trough. Back in Nazareth, Joseph's own crib stood empty, a silent testimony to expectations held, yet not fulfilled.

If Joseph did make a crib under those circumstances, Jesus never slept in it. The unexpected journey to Bethlehem and the enforced exile in Egypt robbed the whole family of their own home and comforts for probably two years. Joseph's crib – such beautiful handiwork left behind. Instead, a feeding trough. Seemingly cold comfort for an infant king. On the night when Jesus was born, did he not deserve more than this?

Of course, Jesus was entitled to the very best the whole earth had to give. Yet with the birth of his own Son, God was showing that when he comes near, it may not be as we expect. 'Many are the plans in a man's heart, but it is the Lord's purpose that prevails' (Proverbs 19:21). For if God were truly to identify himself with us, it could be no corner-cutting exercise. In Jesus he had to see the very best and worst of human experience. On the night that Jesus was born, Jesus took his first share of the worst. When the labour suite was more suited to animal than to human habitation, we know that God had no intention of cushioning his Son from adversity. Jesus' birth paved the way for his life: this was to be no sheltered existence. Words of comfort from a God secluded from affliction would seem like empty platitudes to anyone weighed down with cares. But a God who chooses to spend his first hours on earth helpless in an animal's feeding trough will be sympathetic towards our pain. And this understanding is important in moulding our own expectations of God.

If God is truly to understand me, and still to be perfect and all-powerful, I have to know he has cried tears of grief and ached with the pain of loss. I have to know he's torn at his hair in frustration, and known the effects of physical and mental pain. In addition, could he also understand what it's like to be lonely and hungry? I want to know he's witnessed the results of failure, yet has never put a foot wrong himself; that he's faced the pressure of difficult decisions, yet always made the right choice. I want to know he's seen disappointment, but has never given up hope; that he understands what it's like to be hurt by a friend, yet has never stopped loving.

A bit too much to expect from God, perhaps? Maybe it does seem a tall order. But our reading from Hebrews introduces us to the very human side of Jesus, a man who underwent a complete human experience, yet preserved his perfection throughout. From the nature of his Son's birth, God showed us he would fully involve himself in the very stuff of human existence. Through Jesus he participated in the mundane and the miraculous. His eyes shone love and wept tears. His hand cracked whips and touched lepers.

His words condoned no sin, yet beckoned repentant sinners. His body, anointed by some in love, was beaten by others in hate. This was a real man, living a real life in a real world.

When we begin to grasp that God therefore understands what it's like to be human, it can revolutionise the way we relate to him. Such a perspective of God as seen through Jesus can help us place our confidence in him. No one but the Emmanuel God is there with us in all our circumstances; it is his very presence and understanding that can transform the way we view what is happening to us.

If there is any truth in the story of the crib, there would have come a day when, after returning from exile, the holy family came home to Nazareth. I imagine that one day Joseph would have carried Jesus into his workshop for the first time and shown him the crib. 'I made that for you,' he might have said, 'but it wasn't to be. But I tell you this: when you were laid in that manger on the night you were born, just because it was you, that manger became the finest crib in all the world.'

Prayer

O come, O come, Emmanuel,
God with us,
who shared the highest and lowest of our humanity.
Help me to realise that when you look upon my troubles,
it is with compassionate and sympathetic eyes.
You stooped to touch the same dust I am sometimes laid in.
You have felt the pain my own heart breaks with.
My tears mingle with ones you have already shed.
May your sympathetic heart give mine courage
to face the times when you act in ways outside my own expectations.
Help me to trust you more.
Amen.

12 DECEMBER

UNEXPECTED BAD NEWS

Readings: Luke 2:1-3, 5:1-11, 8:40-56

Joseph lifted his eyes from his work, his concentration momentarily distracted by the sound of increased activity in the street. Stepping out of the workshop he was immediately run into by another villager, streaming with many others like a human wave towards the market place. 'What's going on?' asked the carpenter.

'There's a Roman official in the market place proclaiming a decree from Caesar,' the man replied. 'They want to hold a census.'

Joseph was just about to shut the shop and join the flow, when Mary hurried up to him. 'Oh, Joseph,' she said breathlessly, 'the news is not good for us.'

'What's all this about a census?' asked Joseph.

'Caesar has decreed that everyone in the Empire must be registered. Each person must travel to their town of origin.'

'That's Bethlehem for us. When must we go?' asked Joseph.

'I've just been working it out,' replied Mary anxiously. 'We'll have to travel just about the time the baby's due. Oh, it's such a mess!'

Joseph took Mary in his arms and they stood silent for a time, a stranded rock in the midst of the stream of people who flowed by them towards the market area. So few things seemed to be straightforward about this particular pregnancy. They were just beginning to settle into things. Now uncertainty had come to haunt them again.

'We'll work it out somehow,' Joseph said, seeking desperately to say something of comfort. He was as perplexed as Mary about this seemingly cruel turn of events, and yet something stirred in his mind – in the old scrolls it was written, out of Bethlehem God would bring a 'ruler for Israel'. It would be futile to fight prophecy.

We do not know how or at what stage of the pregnancy Mary and Joseph first heard of the Roman census decree. However this happened, it must have come as a shock to them, when they realised it coincided with the expected timing of Jesus' birth. Concealed within Mary's womb, Jesus would not have been immune from the anxiety she experienced as the impact of the news sunk in. When bad tidings were received, Jesus was right there.

Jesus never escaped the bitter sting of bad news throughout his comparatively short life on earth. During his public ministry he came close to a number of people who faced difficult truths. Take, for example, two very different men: Simon Peter and Jairus. One, a fisherman with no catch, losing a whole night's revenue; the other, a synagogue ruler, losing his daughter through sickness.

For each man there was nothing in the reality of their situation to encourage them. For Simon, the best time to fish had slipped away, just like the fish themselves. He and his companions were now tired and frustrated. Jairus received one of the most devastating pieces of news for any father: 'Your daughter is dead. Why bother the teacher any more?' The final words of those messengers reveal an all-too-common reaction towards God in the face of pain: 'Why bother with God? He's not doing me any favours at the moment. He's let me down.' We feel, like Simon, we've given all we can, yet even this, it seems, is not enough.

Jesus chose to intervene directly at those critical moments for both men. To each he gave an instruction which, considered on the sheer facts, seemed quite ludicrous. Simon received the following command: 'Put out into the deep water, and let down your nets for a catch.' Since when has a carpenter ever been a better judge of fishing than a fisherman? Yet incredibly, Simon obeys. Why? Let him explain in his own words: '. . . because you say so.' Only because of Jesus. Simon was helped, not because he responded to Jesus' logic, but instead because he acknowledged his Lordship.

And what of Jairus? He was a grief-stricken man, having to control himself in front of a large crowd. He had to wait for what seemed an eternity while Jesus conversed with a previously unclean woman, stopping everyone just for her. Jesus then had the apparent audacity to dismiss the fact that Jairus' daughter was now dead, and instructed him instead: 'Don't be afraid; just believe.' Incredibly, like Simon before him, Jairus chose to do just that. There could only be one reason why Jairus refused to give up – Jesus. For I doubt if anyone else could have instilled so much faith with so few words.

The stories of Simon and Jairus are an encouragement to me when life becomes difficult enough to wonder if God is worth believing in. Because, let's face it, there are times when we can doubt God to that extent. And such doubts can often be caused by unexpected bad news. The Bible is a very honest handbook; it does not peddle escapist solutions to life's problems. One verse I seek comfort in at these times is Psalm 112:7: 'He will have no fear of bad news; his heart is steadfast, trusting in the Lord.' The Psalmist doesn't claim that bad news isn't bad. It most certainly can be. He is not saying that bad news doesn't hurt. It does; bad news hurts badly. He is simply saying that at the times when you feel you've nothing left to hold on to, you can still hold on to God. It doesn't matter how bleak or unpromising life may appear: because the Lord is near, life can go on.

In the face of painful truths, which indiscriminately strip away all that is false in us, a simple faith goes a long way. Searching for clever answers to explain life's most difficult moments is a fruitless quest. For to believe in God when there's no reason to believe other than himself alone, defies all logic. That kind of faith can only operate when we realise that God is close by. When there's nothing else to cling on to, we need to know that God's hand is still within reach.

I still have much to learn about this kind of faith. I am also slowly discovering that God does not have to be just a companion in crisis, a last resort for when I'm at my wit's end. Through Mary and Joseph's experiences, I am recognising instead that God is close, not only to share my pain, but also to celebrate my joy.

Cling to the God who is near. As you do, listen for his voice among the others which drown or dismiss it. For when the news is bad, the words which matter most are spoken by the one who was good news for us. When the Light of the world shines nearby, our world takes on a different hue.

Prayer

O come, O come, Emmanuel,
you who are the message of life.
Help me to cling tightly to you
when the day is dark and the news is bad,
knowing that you will not flinch
even if my very life depends on my grip on you.
Encourage me by your presence,
so I will not fear the headlines which threaten to uproot me,
but will instead view them in your light,
still holding fast to your words from centuries past:
'Don't be afraid; just believe.'
Amen.

13 DECEMBER

GOD'S PERFECT TIMING

Reading: Galatians 3:26–4:7

Mary was still feeling crushed by the news of the census. She was frightened by the prospect of an arduous journey, so close to her due date. She had never travelled that far before and stories of thieves and brigands on the lonely country roads only added to her sense of foreboding.

Of all the times for her to have to undertake a journey like this! For Mary the timing couldn't have been worse. She had enjoyed the stability of being first at Elizabeth's and then back in Nazareth. Now that sturdy foundation was crumbling to powder beneath her. Danger, like an evil sneering face, leered at her in her mind's eye.

'If only it could all be at another time,' wished Mary. She knew that it was quite foolish to hope that any decree of Caesar could be repealed. Mary's querulous 'if only' was a symptom of her frustration at the timing of the census. She did not understand how God could allow her to undertake the journey to Bethlehem when she would be nine months pregnant. Had God no idea about antenatal care for mothers and their babies?

Mary's cry of confusion was not the first to be sent heavenwards. And if my life is any yardstick to go by, it has not been the last. Understandable though it was for Mary to question the timing of the journey to Bethlehem, there was no mistake about the place or the time of Jesus' birth. With hindsight, St Paul could see how perfectly scheduled was that divine delivery: 'But when the time had fully come, God sent his Son, born of a woman, born under law, to redeem those under law, that we might receive the full rights of sons' (Galatians 4:4-5). But for Mary, caught up in developments which only caused fear, it was a lesson that events which seemed out of her control remained well within God's.

For the birth of the world's most important baby, God had an appointed place and time. It is perhaps not surprising that the most perfectly timed birth in history produced the person with the most finely poised sense of timing there has ever been. Jesus never allowed time to be his master, but skilfully wove the thread of his life through each day in accordance with his Father's will.

Jesus knew that the timing of his ultimate goal could not be forced upon him. He would not be swayed by the expectations of others. Five times in John's Gospel we are told that Jesus' time 'had not yet come'. He would always distance himself from those who sought to place their human agenda upon him. His rejection of others' time-frames caused consternation in some and anger in others, but Jesus would not be deflected from his appointed mission. And, after several years of waiting, there came a point when 'Jesus knew that the time had come for him to leave this world' (John 13:1). The waiting was over; his final goal was near. His was a ministry beautifully sandwiched between declarations of being on schedule. His first recorded words in Galilee: 'The time has come' (Mark 1:15); his last, knowing that all was completed upon the cross: 'It is finished' (John 19:30). Jesus showed us a God who is in perfect control of time.

Have you, like me, ever caught yourself saying, 'Don't disturb me now, Lord, can't you see my life's already arranged?' We have our schedules and appointments, our deadlines and commitments. Sometimes we feel God interrupts our lives at the most inopportune moments.

The Christmas story is a challenge to our view of time, and the way we choose to interpret it. I am arrested by a telling phrase of Jesus', spoken after one of his declarations that his time had not yet come. Ponder these words: 'For you any time is right' (John 7:6). As ever Jesus exposes the true root of our misunderstanding of time. For him, each moment was appointed by his Father and it had its special place in time. Our problem is that often we do not see these ordained moments, where the magnitude of the event itself far surpasses the actual time it occurs. When Jesus was born, the fact that it might have been, for example, 2am or 4am, was totally eclipsed because above everything else the Messiah had come. In the fuss of misunderstanding God's timing, we may miss the very significance of his actions, and in turn fail to realise that he has come near. Advent invites us to look beyond the actual timing of events to interpret the deeper purposes of God who is always counting the beats of history.

When God comes close, we will sometimes find those deeper purposes cutting right across the plans we have so carefully laid for ourselves. It is a challenge at these times to allow our agenda to yield to his. Perhaps one lesson we really need to learn in life is to synchronise our own watch with God's. For unless we do we will be forever captive to a mind-set which possesses little sense of God's special appointments. Such events will remain only inconveniences for us. But let us instead, like the men of Issachar in 1 Chronicles 12:32, understand the times and the God behind them, who is never too early, never too late, but always on time.

Prayer

O come, O come, Emmanuel,
and by your presence comfort me
that you are in control of time.
Help me realise that history's clock
always remains before you on heaven's wall.
Your master plan is unfolding before you;
as conductor of time, you determine the beats of history.
Enable me to yield to your perfect timing,
to synchronise my life with yours,
no longer clinging to my own agenda,
but seeking first your kingdom.
Open my eyes to look beyond the immediate
to see your deeper purposes.
Lord, my time is yours.
Amen.

14 DECEMBER

HIDDEN TREASURES

Readings: Luke 2:19, 51b

The last few weeks had been a difficult period for Mary. She was weary of the suspicions of her fellow villagers and unhinged by the mood swings which swept her to either extreme, sometimes in the space of the same day. Casting a wary eye over her increased size, she was aware of the noticeable changes in her body. As she lay on her bed, she wondered just how large she would eventually grow.

If she was honest, God had not featured in her thoughts in recent days. Instead it was the biological transformations within her own body which dominated her attention. What peculiar conditions must be weathered by child-bearing women. Men have it so easy!

Suddenly, a delicate ripple, like a caress from a butterfly's wing, fluttered within her abdomen. Mary drew in breath sharply and clasped her hand over the area. Jesus! For the first time she had felt his kick from within. It was a sudden prompt to awareness of his silent presence. Mary sat motionless, all her senses quivering with anticipation, expecting further movement from the baby. But nothing more came. It was almost (as Mary came to wonder) that Jesus had just done enough to remind her that he was there at a time when Mary was not taking notice. It was the first of what would become daily reminders throughout the rest of the pregnancy, drawing her closer to the child she was bearing.

The singer of the Magnificat sat quietly, filled again with exuberant praise for the God who had entrusted his own Son to her body. Then, turning her love inward, she responded to Jesus' opening overture, greeting him with tender words of affection.

Glance at most paintings of Mary and you will see depicted a woman of contemplation. There is often a quiet, thoughtful countenance, as if great, yet hidden, jewels lie just behind her placid exterior. This artistic depiction is true to scripture. In his Gospel narrative, Luke records twice that Mary treasured up many memories of her early days with Jesus, and I have no doubt she would have done the same with recollections of her first pregnancy. One such reminiscence may well have been the first time she felt Jesus move within her. Like Jacob waking to find he'd been dreaming on holy ground (Genesis 28), like Samson's parents realising they'd been conversing with an angel (Judges 13), so Mary would have felt this silent and unexpected reminder of God's hidden presence.

In the original Greek, Luke's description of Mary's recollections links two related thoughts. First, there is the sense of Mary safely guarding her memories of that time. Second, her recollections were a drawing together of thoughts as she actively contemplated past circumstances. Like treasured keepsakes, Mary's memories were pondered to bring into focus the whole picture of these life events.

Like any pregnant woman, Mary would have experienced the deep mystery of building relationship with her unborn child. She would have been conscious of a life within her, separate from herself, yet inextricably linked. She would have been aware of the independence of the foetal Christ, but conscious of his total dependence upon her for security and nourishment. I am sure that this mystery would have been a source of great joy to Mary as she contemplated all that was taking place. For Mary those foetal movements, those sudden promptings of Christ's presence, would have become more frequent as the pregnancy progressed until, one day, unstoppable contractions within her would bring her face to face with Almighty God.

Our minds are a miscellany of memories, archived in ways we'll never understand. Yet stored they are, some within easy reach, others so deeply deposited that only a specific event triggers their recollection. There is enormous power in our memories; they carry the potential to stabilise our lives or to destroy them. Our minds have the capacity for good and bad. Memories of good times with God lay down a foundation of trust in him, strengthening our hidden resources. But I also know that the deliberate harbouring of long-term bitterness, for example, will only bring inner decay.

Our minds are battle zones. If we do not choose to fill our minds with good thoughts of God, the devil will fill them with disparaging ones instead, or else our fleshly desires will push God out altogether. What is not surrendered to God is claimed by the flesh and the devil. God's arch-enemy will remind us of our own failings. He'll draw deliberate attention to times when we've doubted God was there. And in so doing he will destabilise our faith.

Mary's example teaches us to win that battle in our minds by conscious contemplation of how good God is. Mary chose to process her experiences inwardly and come to a clear understanding of what was taking place. This would not only have strengthened her own mind, but would have kept her own view of God accurate. One of the reasons God can seem distant is because we lose sight of who he is. Regular recollection of his nature and dealings with us clarifies our view of him.

It's in the difficult times, when God does seem far away, that we need to draw on the memories he has laid down in our lives; times when God has reminded us in surprising ways that he really is right beside us. It is important to remember that God is not always predictable in the methods he uses to ensure his closeness to us. Who would have expected his mission in Jesus to end on a hill outside Jerusalem? For there we see the ultimate intervention of God to bring us close. This time it was not achieved with a baby's kick, but with a man's writhing body. Through a tortured Christ and a torn curtain, God was breaking back into our world to show that even at the blackest hour, he could still perform a telling act of communication.

Prayer

O come, O come, Emmanuel,
and keep me poised for unexpected encounters with you.
Thank you that you are with me,
even though I may not always be aware of it.
Help me to realise that each place
may be a rendezvous with you.
Forgive me for the times when I have failed
to realise you are there.
In your graciousness,
come to me again in fresh ways.
Strengthen me inwardly
through the recollection of your goodness,
that my eyes would in future be opened wider to see
that your presence is very real.
Amen.

15 DECEMBER

CALLING JESUS NAMES

Readings: Isaiah 9:1-7, Matthew 1:21-23

When it came to thinking about names for their expected child, Mary and Joseph were treading a very different path to most other would-be parents. Not only had they been informed of the sex of the child, but they had also received instruction as to his name. They could not spend time discussing their favourite names for a boy or a girl and deciding on a choice for each sex. All this responsibility had been taken from them. Jesus was a fairly common name, and not one that they disliked, although if they ever did have a son the name James had been in their minds . . .

Every Jew knew the importance in a name, and Mary and Joseph had been clearly reminded of the significance of calling the child-to-come Jesus. What was it the angel had said to Joseph? '. . . Because he will save his people from their sins.' Jesus – 'the Lord saves'. Mary and Joseph knew well the stories of the great saviours from Israel's past – the judges and kings who many times brought the nation back from the brink of destruction. But they were saviours in a national sense. There was something in the angel's words which was hard to understand: '. . . he will save his people from their sins.' Save us from our sins? How would their son do this? It just didn't make sense. The Jews had only ever had one way to make atonement for their sins, and that always involved blood and sacrifice . . .

Jesus was called many names during his time on earth, some complimentary, others definitely not. But it was the identity ascribed to him by the angel at the beginning of his life, in Mary's womb, which was the bottom line in defining who he was and what he had come to do. Jesus' name was signed and sealed in heaven before anyone on earth saw him in the flesh. It was important for it to be this way, for no other name would have been fitting for this particular child with his unique task. In scripture there are seven people whose names are prophesied before their birth.* It is not surprising that Jesus is the seventh of these, seven being symbolic of perfection. As the Bible teaches, his is the name above all others.

The name bestowed upon earth's most precious child underlined supremely his nature and his mission. He was the Lord and he had come to save. At the end of the day, God's Son had come to be a saviour. That was his mission, and every time his name

---

* The seven are: Ishmael (Genesis 16:11), Isaac (Genesis 17:19), Solomon (1 Chronicles 22:9), Josiah (1 Kings 13:2), Cyrus (Isaiah 45:1), John the Baptist (Luke 1:13) and and Jesus (Luke 1:31).

was spoken, that goal was further proclaimed. Jesus was clear in declaring what he had come to do: 'The Son of Man came to seek and to save what was lost' (Luke 19:10). He was a seeker and a saviour. Like a woman sweeping her whole house to find one misplaced coin, like an anxious shepherd scurrying across the fields for one sheep which missed the count, like a loving father with a heart which bleeds for his son to come home, so Jesus came looking. He was and is looking for anyone who has the courage to realise that they have lost their path and need the Way; that they have lived only a lie and need the Truth; that they have squandered their purpose and need the Life. Such is the attitude of the one who acknowledges Christ as Lord as well as Saviour.

Jesus still seeks us. That's part of his very nature. For him, coming close is just part of living up to his name. The woman gets down on her hands and knees to pick up the coin from the corner of the room. The shepherd hoists his missing sheep across his shoulders and joyfully tramps home. The father runs full pelt towards the son when he is seen from afar and takes him in his arms. Jesus cannot search without getting near. To be a saviour is only one aspect of his mission; being a seeker is the other.

What will we call Jesus this Christmas? The words we choose reveal the extent of his involvement in our lives. To call him by his proper name – Lord and Saviour – issues us with a challenge to accept him as first priority in our lives and to give him permission to deal with the sin that is found there.

At Christmas, with all our focus on Jesus as a baby, it is easy to forget just who he really is. If we are to take him seriously this December we must examine carefully how we truly view him. If I am brutally honest, there have been too many occasions when the words I use to speak of Christ are only a smoke screen camouflaging my true response to him, which is observed only deep within my heart. I have called him 'Wonderful', yet have harboured serious doubts as to his benevolence because of bad experiences, the blame for which I have laid squarely at God's door. I have proclaimed him 'Mighty God' in my prayers, yet have wondered if he really is powerful enough to come to my aid. I have named him 'Everlasting Father', yet concerns have been present about how loving I believe God is towards me. I have declared him 'Prince of Peace', while some storm-torn sections of my life are deliberately withheld from his serenity.

Such discrepancies of speech and truth are painful to admit. But if we are to appreciate fully the God who is close, we must remember, like Mary and Joseph, that we don't have the choice of what kind of a God he is. He comes to us as he is. We do not choose his name; we cannot determine his nature. Bringing the way we speak of God into line with the reality of his true nature is not normally an overnight event. In this process God is more concerned with our honesty than our haste. From his perspective, the importance lies in us being on the journey, rather than how far we have travelled. Let us only call him our Lord and Saviour if that is what he truly is. But wherever we are on our journey to that point, as we increasingly understand Jesus through his name, we are grasping more of what Christmas is really all about.

Prayer

O come, O come, Emmanuel,
and help me to recognise
that you are truly One who came to seek and save.
Yet I still need to receive that truth,
for I am often lost and need your rescue.
So, Good Shepherd, come again across the hills and seek me,
for I am one of your flock.
Save me from speaking of you in ways which deny
how I really feel about you.
You desire honesty from me;
help me to display it, particularly this Christmas.
May I not only wonder that you were the baby at Bethlehem,
but worship you as the One with the name above all names.
Amen.

16 DECEMBER

DECISION-MAKING

Readings: 1 Corinthians 2:6-16; Colossians 2:8-10

Periodically the reality of approaching parenthood would hit Mary and Joseph with full force. This time it was triggered by a conversation Mary had with a young mother in Nazareth. Although sympathetic towards Mary, this mother talked at great length about all the changes that motherhood brought. But sadly for Mary, the emphasis was on the negative: the way this woman's baby was inconveniencing her life and the stress caused by the incessant choices to be made. Mary went home feeling that the responsibility for this woman's baby as well as her own was on her shoulders.

Mary and Joseph were keenly aware that big decisions would face them as parents. There would be choices about feeding the baby in the early days, decisions about the timing and style of weaning. Later on would come the plans concerning discipline and education.

The identity of their child did not calm their concerns; on the contrary, it heightened them. For how should you raise God's Son? Who were they to instruct this holy child? Surely he had more to teach them. The consequences of their parental decisions were literally eternal. And now, at the end of the second trimester, the full enormity of these choices was sinking in.

In the face of this future, Mary and Joseph felt quite numb and helpless. At such times, the carefree heart of their youthfulness would flood with the burden of adult responsibility. It was some-times asphyxiating; they longed for the clear air of godly wisdom. That was at the heart of every prayer they uttered about what lay ahead: 'Lord, we need you now more than ever before.'

Walk into any shop selling baby equipment and you can guarantee it will make your head spin in bewilderment. Take prams and buggies, for example. You survey the parking lots of possibilities with trepidation. There are ones with reversible seats, some with hoods, some without. Certain models have swivel wheels, others have only fixed ones. A few all-terrain models have only three wheels and resemble a small, earth-bound hang-glider. Newer models feature a cradle on wheels on which fits the latest make of car seat for ease of transition from vehicle to pram and vice versa. Confused? You will be, and we haven't even begun to consider the range of rain-shields, cosy-toes and other accessories . . .

Prospective parents in our modern age face these kinds of choices. Deeper than the practical options for prams or buggies comes the choice of child-rearing philosophies. And beyond all of these are the very principles we hold that govern our lives. What kind of wisdom is guiding us?

Mary and Joseph were spared the task of choosing buggies, baby monitors, car seats and the like. But the deeper issues were very real for them. They must have struggled in their decisions regarding how to bring up Jesus. There would have been influences from their own upbringing, as well as pressure from those around them.

St Paul's heartfelt advice to the Colossian Church was that they should not succumb to worldly philosophies (Colossians 2:8). This itinerant apostle came across many kinds of philosophies on his travels and knew how easy it was to be taken captive by them. Paul warned us of the seductive suction of anything that would draw us from the influence of God's wisdom.

In all the decisions Mary and Joseph had to take, God was with them in a remarkable way. Jesus, the very wisdom of God, was personally present to them. They were to learn that the God who so intricately wove his Son together in Mary's womb was ready to grant all the wisdom they could ever need for parenting and life in general. Decision-making can be a lonely business. Advent teaches us to remember the Counsellor whose wisdom is only a prayer away.

The longer I go on in life, the more I recognise my need of God. Every decision is a junction, sometimes of multiple paths. To every choice is a consequence. When I consider the totality of permutations which result from my ability to choose, it is a sobering and frightening thought.

There is encouragement from Advent's message as we face life's decisions: we have a God who is no stranger to this. The following story helps to illustrate this. It was a summer day in 1937 and John Griffith, the controller of a railway drawbridge over the Mississippi River, had taken Greg, his 8-year old son, with him to work. At midday John raised the drawbridge to allow several ships to pass underneath, while he and Greg ate their lunch on the observation deck. Just after 1pm, John heard the distant whistle of the Memphis Express and, looking around for Greg, he reached for the lever to lower the drawbridge. To his horror, John suddenly realised that his son had fallen into the massive gears that operated the bridge. Greg's left leg was caught in the cogs of the main gears.

As the sound of the Memphis Express grew louder, fear and panic gripped John's mind as he frantically searched for options. There were but two: either to sacrifice his son to spare the passengers on the train, or sacrifice them to save his son. With his face buried in his left hand, John grabbed the lever in his right, forcing it into place to lower the bridge.

Heaven only knows the anguish John Griffith experienced in those fateful moments and the years of anguish that must have followed. I am awed at his courageous action, all the more so because I have a young son. Call me weak, but I do not think I could have done what he did if I were in the same situation. Because of this, I stand in even greater awe of our Father God who deliberately chose to give up his only Son to be born and die among us. He did not have to send him, but he made that choice. He faced the tough options; he knew the bottom line. He never shirked his responsibility; he didn't pass the buck. He weighed up all the options, but there was only one way. For to reconcile humankind to a holy God takes someone who has shared the life of both.

So now, whenever we face an important choice, let's remember with thankfulness the presence with us of a God who, when it came to the crunch, faced the toughest decision in the history of the world, and judged right. As we look to him for his wisdom, how can he fail to instruct us?

Prayer

O come, O come, Emmanuel,
the wisdom of God from ages past.
Draw near to me when choices are many and answers are few.
Help me to rely on you.
Protect me from the discouragement caused by what I don't know;
help me to trust you because of what I know of you.
Thank you that you chose to send your Son;
how that must have torn at your heart.
Encourage me to ask for the wisdom of your mind
given with the tenderness of your heart.
Amen.

TAKING THINGS FURTHER

Summary

As the months passed and Mary moved into the second trimester of her pregnancy with Jesus, much of what took place seemed more routine and mundane. The rush of extraordinary events surrounding Jesus' conception was over, and life fell back into a semblance of normality. Our own walk with God has parallels with this: there are moments when it seems a window opens and the grace of God floods into our lives, only to close up and that glimpse of eternity is gone. Advent is a time when we can reflect on how ordinary moments are still grace-filled opportunities. Of course, preparations for the birth of Jesus began in earnest: Mary making clothes and Joseph a crib. There was the growing realisation of changing priorities and the enormous responsibilities of parenthood. Mary and Joseph's experiences provide us with a good opportunity to consider our own priorities and the place the Lord has among them.

And just when life seemed settled came the news of the census and its implications for the holy couple. A long journey now lay ahead, just around the time of delivery. It was a frightening prospect. Christmas, a time when we celebrate good news, is actually a key occasion to learn lessons of how our faith in Christ assists us when bad news strikes. As Mary and Joseph found, the presence of Christ was there with them, giving them the reassurance they needed in God's plans for them all.

Discussion questions

9. Spend some time praying and reflecting about new ways in which the Lord may want you to serve him in your locality. Remember that to serve those in need is to serve Christ.

10. What does it mean to abide in Jesus as the true Vine? What could you do to strengthen your attachment to him?

11. Choose an appropriate selection of passages from the Gospels and from them identify the human experiences Jesus would have undergone. What encouragement can this give us because of Jesus' understanding of our humanity?

12. Pick some stories of trouble, grief or hardship which have been in the news recently. Pray the Lord's presence and peace into those situations. If you are in a group, allow any member to share a piece of bad news they may have recently received and pray for them. If you are on your own and you have recently received bad news, ask a trusted friend to pray for you.

13. Recall any situations that come to mind where your sense of timing differed from God's. What happened in the end? What did you learn from these experiences?

14. In a group setting, give members at least a week's notice to prepare to share some aspect of their walk with the Lord. It might be an answered prayer, a Bible verse that spoke powerfully to them, or some other encouragement or lesson learned. Then come together and savour one another's stories. Spend some time afterwards praying for one another in the light of what was shared.

15. Make as exhaustive a list as you can of all the names which Jesus is called in the Bible. You may be surprised by how many there are! Discuss together the significance behind the names you have listed and turn your thoughts into prayer.

16. What factors help you to take important decisions? What role does and should our faith play in this?

THIRD TRIMESTER
17-25 DECEMBER

17 DECEMBER

NEW PRIORITIES

Readings: Galatians 2:20; Philippians 3:4b-11

Ever since Gabriel's words inaugurated her pregnancy, Mary's lifestyle had changed. At first, each change seemed small, almost imperceptible and of little consequence in the whole picture. But now, looking back, the effect of her pregnancy was obvious. These changes had become permanent features of her life as the reality of the pregnancy set in. Mary was extra careful about what she ate and she took more exercise than usual. She tried not to lift anything heavy and spent many hours sewing for the impending arrival.

But these outward changes were just signs of the more fundamental transformation going on inside. For even while Jesus was still unborn, the very way Mary thought was experiencing revolution. First in her relationship with Joseph, and now with the realisation of Jesus' forthcoming birth, Mary was learning vital lessons about how her life intersected the lives of others. The decisions she took had massive implications for those close to her. She was not a free agent; she could not simply do whatever she wanted. She had a husband and a son; both needed her. Mary's priorities were changing.

It was clear to Mary that, once Jesus was born, her priorities would be different from those she held with Joseph before the Annunciation. Motherhood would change so many areas of her life. There would be commitments of time, emotional energy, prayer and instruction. How strange that one so small should generate so much change!

Mary was grateful for the time to ponder and pray about what lay ahead. She knew that living up to these new priorities would be a good deal harder than the contemplation of them. And yet she felt a quiet confidence that God would help her as she made these vital adjustments.

Recently my sister-in-law showed me a wristband she had bought for one of her children. Inscribed on it were the letters WWJD. What did they stand for? 'What Would Jesus Do?' The wristband was a prompt for that child to realise that what Jesus thinks is an important factor in our decision-making.

Becoming a Christian involves a change in our priorities. Jesus takes centre stage. No longer can we live only for ourselves, as if there were no God. Christmas has shown us that God is truly among us. We cannot pretend he is not looking. We cannot behave as though he were distant and remote. As we go on in our lives as Christians, old ways have to go; a new set of values is embraced. The Apostle Paul succinctly summed up his own experience of this in these words: 'I no longer live, but Christ lives in me. The life I live in the body, I live by faith in the Son of God, who loved me and gave himself for me' (Galatians 2:20). And in today's passage from Philippians, Paul enlarges on the complete turnabout he experienced after conversion. He details for us the new priorities which came into his life. Trust in external regulations of religion was out; reliance on the grace of God was in. Paul turned his back on religious kudos to embrace his true identity in Christ. This was a radical reordering of his private world, a massive upheaval in his personal landscape. So deep was the change in priorities in his life, that he considered some of what came before as refuse. Now he had his eyes firmly fixed on Jesus.

Paul's life is an important example of how the presence of Jesus should affect the way we think and live. We owe much to Paul for the honesty with which he opened his heart to us, and granted us a precious glimpse of powerful personal change.

It is only when the ways of God clash with our ways that we discover the depth of our commitment to him. It sometimes takes very little to scratch away at the surface of our faith, and what is revealed beneath can be a very different shade.

If I am to take matters of faith seriously, I cannot escape the spotlight of tough questions. Because of Jesus, what is different in my life? Is my thinking shaped by him? Are my actions pleasing to him? If I am to know the closeness of Christ, I must be willing to accept the changes that accompany this. A true commitment is reflected in the priorities which flow out from it.

The new priorities which Mary and Joseph had to embrace as they anticipated the arrival of Jesus remind us of the new priorities we adopt as we follow Christ. Before we were Christians, we were perhaps less troubled by moral dilemmas, more prepared to fall in with the existing climate of opinion. Now we face such issues personally, struggling to know how we should put Jesus first.

One of the subtlest traps that we fall into as believers in Christ is to allow ourselves to be convinced that a Christ-centred lifestyle is just one of many options; we may choose it occasionally, but it is not an absolute. Living as we do in a 'pick and mix' society, it is all too easy to fall prey to this way of thinking.

Commitment to Jesus is absolute and keeping him as our top priority is easier when we consider his closeness. Many a time I will think twice about sin when I realise that Jesus is close enough to see, not only my actions, but also what is in my mind. Although I accept Christ as my righteous judge, it is not fear that forces me away from sin. It is rather that I am enticed towards righteousness because, as I consider Christ's closeness and sheer goodness, I am convinced that I cannot commit sin in the presence of one so holy. His own purity inspires my own. I think this is what the Apostle John wanted to convey when he wrote: 'No one who is born of God will continue to sin, because God's seed remains in him; he cannot go on sinning, because he has been born of God' (1 John 3:9).

And when I think of his closeness, it becomes a powerful stimulus for me to pursue righteousness. He looks upon me as a loving parent, encouraging his child towards new achievements. He is eager for our godliness; he is jealous for our hearts.

It is not easy to put Jesus first. In today's world, where trust seems cheap, commitment is not a fashionable word. But Christmas is the first light of God's most tangible commitment to us. A total involvement in our world, in our joy, in our pain, even in our physiology. For that wondrous night, when angels looked down to behold the birth of Christ, heaven had temporarily lost a Son, but the world had forever gained a Saviour. God's commitment to us has never failed. When we consider his gift at Christmas, how can we not return him to his rightful place in our lives?

Prayer

O come, O come, Emmanuel,
the Lord of all the earth.
Help me to recognise that you are not an option,
you are an absolute;
and that my life will never be richer than when I place you first.
Reassure me of your presence at those times
when I struggle to give you your rightful place.
Remind me of your great commitment to me,
that in the light of that I might freely offer my heart back to you.
Amen.

18 DECEMBER

WAITING FOR IT ALL TO HAPPEN

Reading: 2 Peter 3:8-9

Mary knew that she was into the last months of her pregnancy. What a journey it had been! For her, the end was in sight – the end, that is, of the pregnancy; the beginning, of course, of Jesus' life on earth.

Increasingly she was conscious of a real desire for the birth to be over. Joseph had to encourage her to be patient. He had seen how her itchy feet only led to an anxious heart.

Mary could not help her feelings of wanting it all to happen. The waiting was not easy, particularly with all the pressures they seemed to be facing as a family. Why did time move so slowly? She knew that in many ways this period of waiting should be easier than most. 'Nine months is nine months,' was how Joseph put it. This time of waiting at least had a definite end point and outcome, and she was aware that others did not always have such luxuries. And there would be times in her life when she would face these same difficulties. 'Please give me patience to trust you, Lord,' Mary prayed.

The hands of the clock never turn slower than for those who wait, and especially for those who wait alone. In our society, waiting is considered purposeless and unproductively passive. We want things quickly. Pandering to this 'now or never' mentality, a 24-hour telephone bank recently ran an advertising campaign with the slogan: 'Don't you just hate queues?' while a credit card company slogan ran, 'Take the waiting out of wanting'. We are slaves to the immediate.

Such a mind-set spills over into our view of God in relation to waiting. Our clamorous nature can reduce God to a tentative, risk-avoiding slow-coach, always lagging behind us. It is easy to become impatient with God, especially when we think we can see the best way forward, and our pleas for his guidance seem to have gone unnoticed. Waiting for God is unfashionable in our world. Yet impatience with God's apparent slowness has probably led more people into the right things at the wrong time than anything else. And the same event, placed within two different time-frames, acquires dramatically altered significance.

Perhaps the hardest sort of waiting occurs when we know neither the final outcome, nor the limit to our waiting time. During a period of unemployment, my life seemed to be characterised by a permanent cascade of overlapping periods of waiting. I would send off an application form . . . then wait. I would send a speculative letter . . . then wait. Sometimes silence was my only answer to these inquiries. The arrival of the post has never been greeted with more hopefulness than during that time. Yet how many times my hope was dashed by a letter of rejection, or no reply at all. In that waiting, there were no guarantees or deadlines for success; it seemed an indefinite trial of faith and patience.

The Bible does not grant us information about how long we must wait for certain things in our lives. Instead it encourages us to wait with expectation (Psalm 5:3), hope (Psalm 33:20) and with patience (Psalm 37:7). We are not awaiting assistance from just anyone. When we look to the Lord to come to our aid, we are appealing to the highest court in the world.

It is our perception of time, captive as we are within its confines, which causes us such angst. Our reading for today grants us God's outlook on time: 'With the Lord, a day is like a thousand years and a thousand years are like a day.' Contrary to what we may think, God is never slow in anything he does. Any delay we detect on his part is due to a deeper work he is involved in.

In my own trials of waiting while unemployed, I was tempted towards adopting a negative view of God. It was easy to think, 'He isn't out of a job, and I'm the one doing all the waiting.' At that time and since, one encouragement has meant more to me than anything else. My own view of waiting was transformed when I realised that I have a companion in it. God is waiting, too. In fact, waiting is a partnership between us. I await God's intervention in my life, as he in turn awaits my continuing faithfulness towards him.

Simone Weil once said, 'Time is God's waiting as a beggar for our love.' God is like the father in Jesus' parable of the prodigal son. He is searching the horizon for any sign of the boy who left home. That son, who couldn't wait to live a life without his father, returned home through shame and disgrace, to discover that his father never stopped waiting to share life again with his son.

So just when I start to despair that God may have left me 'on hold' for ever, I remember him as that waiting father, owning everything except the love I refuse to give to him. And as my own heart is broken by his patience towards me, I realise that this gift of time, which I have so often despised, was given that I might demonstrate my love for him. 'Since ancient times no one has heard, no ear has perceived, no eye has seen any God besides you, who acts on behalf of those who wait for him' (Isaiah 64:4).

Prayer

O come, O come, Emmanuel,
and partner me when the silence of waiting is long,
and the answers are few.
Comfort me with your companionship
when I am tired of being 'on hold'.
Help me to trust you when the future is uncertain
and I long for things to be sorted.
Thank you that you ascribe a perfect time for everything
and that, as I trust your will for me,
you will satisfy my restlessness with your very self.
Amen.

19 DECEMBER

YOU CAN'T HIDE GOD

Readings: Matthew 5:14-16; 13:44-46

It had been some weeks now since Mary had last seen her waistline. There was some concern in her about whether she would see it again following the birth. Although she hated making comparisons, she couldn't help thinking of the mothers she had seen in Nazareth who had recovered their figures within weeks of childbirth. How she hoped she would be like them!

There was no disguising her pregnancy now; even under her loose clothes the knowing eye could detect the contours of expectancy. Mary knew it was time for explanations. She felt a strange mix of emotions. Part of her had been desperate for weeks to speak of what was happening; this precious life of God within her had to be proclaimed. And yet, too, she felt anxiety, imagining the reaction of sceptical villagers.

Yet the true work of God must be made known. Why, it was three months ago now that Zechariah's and Elizabeth's son was born. That was a miracle attested by the people. There was no reason why her story shouldn't be believed . . .

Mary wanted to do all she could to nourish Jesus. She kept up daily exercise and took what she hoped was sufficient daily rest. She felt very healthy, both physically and emotionally. There were days when she woke, feeling ready to take on any challenge the world might throw at her. She knew it was something to do with the pregnancy. The life of Jesus within her was nourishing her at a greater depth than she was nourishing him. His hidden, silent work was continuing. Mary continued to marvel at it. Less than three months left; time was moving so quickly now.

The longer the pregnancy progressed, the more Mary had to come to terms with the fact that it would not last for ever. Unstoppable biological forces would one day expel Jesus from her womb, but before that time, Mary had to come to terms with the idea that one day she would have to offer him to the world as its Saviour. There was no way she could keep Jesus all to herself. Her increasing size was a constant reminder that Jesus must leave her body for the sake of the world. Mary could not hold onto him; she had to give him away that others would be served.

Mary's experience mirrors our own in that we are not selfishly to protect the Lord's presence with us. We have no monopoly on him. God longs for the nourishment of his presence in us by his Spirit to be shared with others. As that much-uttered phrase reminds us, 'Christmas is for giving'.

Sadly we can be slow to learn about sharing Jesus with others. Some consider faith to be private, consigning the presence of Christ to a file marked 'personal and confidential'. Much more common, though, is failing to share Jesus because we don't realise that what we have is too good to keep to ourselves. Perhaps we feel we will run dry if we give. We fall into a 'run-of-the-mill' faith: gone is the excitement of early belief; we become tired of expecting answered prayer. Quiet times happen, but they are a perfunctory brief exchange between casual acquaintances rather than an intimate dialogue shared by close friends. Faith becomes familiar, somehow ordinary. We might convince ourselves that we would never let our faith deteriorate in that way. But it can happen, even to the extent of denying the true state of our faith and feigning greater spirituality than we feel. In contrast, the latter months of Mary's pregnancy help us to see how a nurtured faith will clearly reveal the presence of Christ in our lives.

How precious is Jesus to us? Tucked neatly among some of his most famous parables, Jesus himself frames two images of the worth of his kingdom. In each picture there is a discovery of hidden treasure so valuable, it's worth more than anything the finder possesses. The point is clear: Jesus' kingdom is just like that. Hidden deep within our hearts, its value surpasses all else in our lives.

I have no problem acknowledging the hidden work of Christ within. But it is a different matter to place its importance above everything else. Part of the problem is that we imbibe from the world an improper attitude towards individual worth. When we read in the newspaper that someone is personally worth £100 million, what does this really mean? Are the rich worth more than the poor? According to the insurance company with whom I have a policy, the value of my life is determined on a yearly basis and tends to increase with inflation! Is this the true measure of my life's worth?

Christmas helps us get to grips with issues like these. Mary deeply treasured her relationship with Jesus. It was a most precious thing: she was submitted to his will for her. The effect of her attitude towards and nourishing of him was seen in her – physically, as she grew in size as well as in spiritual terms. And through all of this, Mary learned to appreciate how precious she was to God. Here was a beautiful reciprocity: Mary treasuring the presence of Christ with her; Mary receiving her true worth through him.

Our lives, too, can reflect this poignant exchange of worth. If we consider Advent, we need never be in doubt as to the value God places on us. Christ left a perfect world to dwell in a sin-torn one. He compressed deity inside a human womb, confined it within skin and bone. And when, thirty years later, he hung on a cross and died, it was our name he carried on his lips, our sin borne within that body. Christ had come to make sacrifice on the earth: his the oblation, ours the redemption. A costly price? Most definitely, and one worth sharing both with those who are already Christians and those who are not. Let us nurture our faith this Advent, and in so doing we will receive precious acknowledgement from the God who gave his Son for us, paying what he thought we were worth.

Prayer

O come, O come, Emmanuel,
and help me grasp just how much I am really worth.
May I base my opinions on what you think
and not be swayed by the world's standards,
which are often so far from yours.
May I wonder again this Christmas at the treasure which is Christ
and grant me the words and the wisdom to convey his worth,
for I pray in his name.
Amen.

20 DECEMBER

CHANGING TIMES

Reading: Philippians 2:1-11

The time had come for Mary and Joseph to pack for the journey to Bethlehem. They had precious little space within the saddle-bags of their donkey and had to be ruthless in deciding what was packed and what was not. The couple lost track of the number of items they hoped to squeeze in but had finally to discard. Resignation to reality was their only option every time.

When at last they stood and looked at the bags, every seam groaning under the strain, the full impact of change finally hit them. For an uncertain length of time ahead, their home would be carried on the back of a donkey. When wrapped like this, the sum total of their lives made small parcels indeed.

This was certainly change, but was it change for the best? Mary and Joseph did not find it easy to accept that there was anything positive about this current stage of events. It was yet another hurdle, another strain. The personal cost to them was rising. When they finally set out on the road to Bethlehem, they were saying goodbye, not just to the security of their own home, but to their life together as a twosome. For when they next saw Nazareth, it would be with a son. As his earthly guardians waved goodbye to their own home, the Messiah himself was just days away from leaving the uterine cocoon which had shielded him for the past nine months.

There is a small percentage of people who live only for change, hankering after the latest fad. If you, like me, are not like this, welcome to the majority. Most of us need time and space to adopt change. We are lovers of the *status quo*, clinging to what we know. Change frightens us because of what lies ahead, or leaves us with regret for what must be left behind. We struggle to embrace the new, still conscious of the pain of the old. We sometimes underestimate the depth of bereavement experienced during a process of change. The former was familiar, safe. The new is not always so inviting.

The Christmas story brings us great encouragement when we experience a time of change. Our reading from Philippians presents us with a God who understands what change is all about. In fact, he was willing to effect the greatest change ever witnessed in all history – from Almighty God of heaven to a helpless human baby on earth. You can't get much more of a contrast than that. And God was not masterminding this change from afar, only remotely affected by its consequences. Instead he himself was at the very heart of the change. Christmas was about the incarnation of his very self. It was a change with long-term implications, not just during the life of Jesus on earth, but for all time, because his mission would touch all of eternity. In Jesus, God was the master of change. By his own incarnation God changed the destiny of humankind for all who accept him. The greatest change ever to occur involved God becoming Emmanuel. How much more will he be with us in our own times of change?

Christmas challenges us to ask what God may want to do in us and through us during a time of change. His presence with us at such times is not without purpose. We may find ourselves learning new approaches to life. Mary and Joseph may well have been confused by their journey to Bethlehem. But they were to learn that God's spotlight was already arching towards that town. All the prophecies from centuries past were rapidly converging on a simple stable where a history-making and history-splitting child would be born.

In a time of change we must be prepared to give as well as to gain. This was God's example in Christ. During a period of unemployment, I was desperate to gain the satisfaction of work again. God, however, was keen to show me that I could use this time to give in ways which were much more difficult while in full-time employment: giving of my time to people; lending a listening ear; sharing in prayer for someone in need; being available during the day. Finding this so rewarding, I wondered how many times relationships had been sidelined due to the demands of work.

This period of change for me could have been viewed very negatively. Unemployment is not much of a progression in the eyes of the world. I have learned, however, that God's incarnation should revolutionise how we approach the whole subject of change. If we are to follow his example we must wave goodbye to status-seeking agenda, and instead shake the hand of the servant-hearted attitude. Some changes we choose or are forced to experience may not appear to be development for us as the world sees it. But if our priorities lie in God's purposes, then his presence assures us that it is his perspective that counts. In our times of transition, let us draw encouragement from the God who understands change, and gives stability through his own unchanging nature.

Prayer

O come, O come, Emmanuel,
into my times of change where foundations are shaking
and priorities are shifting.
Stand alongside as that unchangeable Rock
and be the stability I need at this time.
Thank you that you understand the difficulties associated with change,
and you are the master of it.
Amen.

21 DECEMBER

ON THE MOVE

Readings: Exodus 13:20-22; 40:34-38

Half-way into their journey to Bethlehem, the strain began to take its toll on Mary and Joseph. Wearied by a whole day's travel, they would seek refuge for the night in a wayside inn, yet could not settle well in a strange place. Mary was finding sleep particularly difficult because of her advanced state of pregnancy. Jesus' unseen movements and her increased size meant that comfort was the last word she would use to describe her night times.

Both Mary and Joseph felt they were part of an 'in-between' existence, on the move and unsettled. It was particularly hard for them at this most critical junction of their lives when they would have sacrificed much for a strong sense of stability. They knew that it was in their hands to make home wherever they chose to tie up their donkey and unpack their bags. But practically this was easier said than done. How can you relax and settle when you're far from home and don't fully know when you will return? No matter how much their minds acknowledged they should try to make the best of their situation, their hearts trailed miserably behind.

It was an anxious time as well, because in those parts you could never be assured of a safe passage. With a good proportion of the populace on the road because of the census, Joseph was especially concerned that the activities of brigands would also increase. He was no trained fighter, but he had made room in their luggage for some choice tools to use as weapons if the need arose. And so they journeyed on, thankful that at least they were together, but longing for the opportunity to spend more than one night in the same place.

The journey to Bethlehem was indeed an anxious time for the holy family. If we were accorded a privileged glimpse inside Mary's womb at that time, I wonder if we would have witnessed the foetal Christ, stretching upwards and hearing the anxious heartbeat of his perturbed mother. We know that unborn babies can keenly sense their mother's emotions, and in some measure Jesus would have been aware of any anxiety in Mary at this important time.

I am struck by how many people experience times of being 'in-between' – caught in a twilight world, having left something behind without yet embracing the new. Like living in the white space between the last line of one chapter and the title of the next. Such times can be very unsettling, a loosening of our foundational soil, bringing a reluctance to put down roots because of the uncertainty of what lies ahead. We can feel caught, paralysed into indecision because we cannot foresee the implications of what we may choose to do. We do not want to take a decision only to find that, as the future opens up, it proves to clash with the path we have chosen.

Mary and Joseph's 'in-between' experience was a small reflection of what the whole Israelite nation endured for their 40 years of wandering in the wilderness. Chapter 33 of the Book of Numbers lists all the different locations where they pitched camp during that time – no less than 40 are chronicled. An average rate of one relocation a year. Considering that a move is one of the most stressful events we face in our lives, we can only imagine how those Israelites must have felt, being continually on the move with little sense of permanence about their lives. They knew for certain that Egypt was a thing of the past, but with no Promised Land in sight, we can understand the extreme frustrations they experienced.

One big issue in transitional periods of our lives is that of friendships. Change sometimes places great strain on even long-standing relationships. When friends become separated by distance, they may drift apart. Even when a change of location is not involved, friendships may be affected through one side experiencing an 'in-between' phase. The unsettling effects that person feels within themselves can spill outwards in their relationships to others.

Good friends who remain strong and loyal through transitional times are highly prized. Ruth was one such biblical character. Faced with the option of separating from her widowed mother-in-law, she would have none of it, preferring to accompany Naomi to Israel and live there. 'Don't urge me to leave you or to turn back from you. Where you go I will go, and where you stay I will stay' (Ruth 1:16). Few are those who enjoy the privilege of such friends.

Christmas helps us remember that God came among us. His presence does not depend on geography, nor is it affected by our experience of 'in-between' chapters in our life. Our readings from Exodus encourage us because in that most transitional period in the life of God's ancient people, he was right there among them. In cloud by day and fire by night, God's presence was clearly visible in all the travels of the Israelites. His constant presence remained in stark contrast to the transient nature of each campsite.

What in our lives seems to be in a state of flux? Are we living in an 'in-between' time? This does not have to be an isolating experience for us. This Christmas, remember the God who travelled in a womb from Nazareth to Bethlehem, accompanying Mary and Joseph on their journey. And remember that he is the same God, who centuries earlier shrouded himself in cloud and fire to demonstrate to his people, then and now, that though their destination is not in sight, his presence with them is not in doubt.

Prayer

O come, O come, Emmanuel,
accompany me through each chapter of my life,
wherever it may take me.
Thank you that you are not confined by geography or time,
but promise your presence in all circumstances.
Guide me as you did your people of old,

that by night or day I would know you are close,
even if my destination is not yet revealed.
Amen.

22 DECEMBER

O LITTLE TOWN

Reading: Micah 5:1-6

As the days passed, Mary and Joseph grew wearier and more travel-stained. Mary was becoming increasingly uncomfortable atop the donkey and Joseph's now blistered feet gave him painful reminders of their presence with every step. Their hearts, however, were lifted through a conversation with a fellow traveller who informed them that Bethlehem would be reached by nightfall.

And so it was that by late afternoon Mary and Joseph looked up across the fields to see the houses on the outskirts of Bethlehem, perched upon its mountain ridge. A thin thread of populace wound its way down the road from the town. Bethlehem was bracing itself for a big influx of visitors.

It seemed to Joseph such a strange destination for him and Mary and their child. This small town, little known save for its famous ancestor David, was about to become the birthplace of another king. Bethlehem would never be the same, and neither would the world. But for the moment, the eyes of heaven were fastened on that small Israelite town.

Joseph had done a great deal of thinking on the journey from Nazareth. He was trying to assimilate it all: Mary's conception, the census, their journey. And as he relived their story, he could see the great author behind the script. Now, as he raised his eyes to the hilltop town ahead, the words of an ancient prophet fluttered through his mind: 'But you, Bethlehem Ephrathah, though you are least among the rulers of Judah, from you will come one who will be ruler over my people Israel.'

Would we have ever heard of Bethlehem were it not for Christmas? The holy nativity changed for ever the destiny of that town. Bethlehem's fame was firmly secured in the annals of history that night. But before Christ came, there was nothing too remarkable about the place. We are right to sing 'O little town' in the words of that carol. The prophet Micah spoke of Bethlehem being 'least among the clans of Judah'. But for his incarnation, his opening night, Bethlehem was God's choice of venue. He set it firmly as a landmark for all the world. Bethlehem is on our map today because from ancient times it was on God's map.

One aspect of the Christmas story is God's choice to fill the ordinary with his presence. Young and inexperienced, Mary and Joseph were given the responsibility of bringing up the world's most precious child. Before they were chosen they were not famous. Only centuries later, when we look back to the original script of Christmas, do we ascribe renown to the main characters. And the ordinary town of Bethlehem received a special touch of heaven when Mary and Joseph brought the very presence of Christ within its perimeter. For those with the discernment to realise, this moment changed the spiritual climate of that place.

There is encouragement here for all who have lost hope that God brings good out of dead-end situations. Christmas shows us a God who took an ordinary town that was going nowhere and put it on the map. In our own experience, we may feel trapped by a dead-end relationship – one with no future; a dead-end job – one with no prospects; a dead-end town – one with no life; a dead-end church – one with no vision. Christmas helps us remember that dead-ends may not be final. It introduces the possibility of breakthrough into our thoughts. It breathes the life-giving oxygen of hope into an asphyxiated prayer life. The presence of Christ with us forms the context within which we should view our circumstances. Recognising he is with us when we feel at a dead-end is the starting point for understanding how we might move on.

Some time ago the church my wife and I were attending went through a difficult period, coinciding with the long process of finding a new minister. The congregation was visibly tired, without leader or vision. At that time a friend from the church publicly shared a dream he had had many years earlier, through which he believed God was speaking. In the dream he stood in a field that had been devastated by a storm. This, he felt, was symbolic of the church's difficulties. Then into the picture came a beautiful stained glass window Nativity scene, with the glory of God all around it. Our friend believed that as the congregation turned to the Lord, his glory would again be revealed. There was a strong sense that this would be fully seen at a future Christmas. Inspired by this, a member of the congregation felt that it was right, that coming Christmas, to create a large printed silk hanging depicting Christmas scenes within a stained glass window, flanked to the right and left by many golden angel wings and two Bible verses about God's glory. The gold was symbolic of the longing of people's hearts for God's glory to return. The striking artwork was a powerful reminder that Christmas shows us a God whose presence with us includes those difficult dead-end situations.

We need reminders like this because being at a dead-end inevitably leads us to believe that life is better elsewhere: that it's time to give up a relationship; time to get another job; that another town would be a better place to live; that there are healthier, livelier churches than our own. We may lose heart, feel unable to believe that our present experience could ever change. Such thoughts keep us focused on our current circumstances and prevent us asking what the Lord may want to do in them and through them.

God's solutions to our dead-ends are not for us to choose, but acknowledging his presence opens us to the creativity of his plans. His presence with us may provide a way out of our predicament or it may help us so transform our situation that it no longer seems a dead-end. As we turn to the Lord we realise that he alone has the real answers. In many ways, he is the one 'dead-end' it's good to come across – once we're with him, we won't want to go anywhere else!

So in those times when we feel we're going nowhere, let's remember the little town that God put on the map. As the holy family came within Bethlehem's outskirts, so in the words of the old carol, 'in thy dark streets shineth the everlasting light'. The spiritual climate was changing, for those with the sensitivity to notice. We too will sense the same in our own lives, for now, just as much as then, God is the one who turns the backyards of Bethlehem into hallowed ground.

Prayer

O come, O come, Emmanuel,
and so inhabit the places in my life
where I feel I'm going nowhere
that I find you alone have the answers for my situation.
May I run into your arms at such times,
knowing they have always held me
and always will.
Calm me with your reassurance
that your plans for me are good,
and that to be with you is to be in the best place.
Amen.

23 DECEMBER

A WARM WELCOME?

Readings: Luke 2:4-7; 7:36-50

By the time Mary and Joseph arrived in Bethlehem, darkness like a thick, black cloak was beginning to envelop the sky. A cold wind had buffeted them for the last hour, making a warm room the desire uppermost in the minds of that weary couple.

Increasingly severe contractions were affecting Mary, drawing in her breath in sharp gasps. The donkey ride had almost certainly accelerated the onset of labour and Mary's anxious glances in Joseph's direction only intensified his resolve to find them accommodation swiftly.

They had been told of three lodging establishments in Bethlehem, but it soon became clear that they had chosen a particularly bad time to arrive. The first two inns were bursting with the sudden influx of visitors, coming to be registered. Both innkeepers were out of breath and out of patience (though not out of pocket) and gave Joseph short shrift, telling him to try another establishment. Protestations from the carpenter about Mary's condition cut no ice at all with them.

It was with considerable desperation that Joseph led their donkey with Mary towards the final inn. The deeply furrowed brow and vexed expression of the innkeeper told the same story as before, but Joseph was too anxious for Mary to be pushed aside this time and his persistence paid off. Although there was no room in the main building, the innkeeper said he would let them stay in the cave at the back, which was used as a stable. It wasn't comfortable, and it wasn't that clean, but at least it was warm. 'Take it or leave it,' was the innkeeper's final offer. 'We'll take it,' said Joseph.

So it was that the couple and their donkey entered that stable, unlikely room companions for the night. Darkness had now drawn the final hem of its cloak across the sky. The stage was set. It was not the kind of scenery Mary and Joseph would have chosen, but then the script was not theirs. From the wings of the earth's great stage, the Messiah was about to make his entrance.

There is a painting by the Dutch artist Breugel occasionally called 'The Numbering' which depicts the census in Bethlehem. The work, completed in 1566, is typical of the artist, the canvas strewn with people frozen in their daily activity. To the left of the picture, a disorderly huddle of travellers in front of a building patiently waits to be registered. In the foreground a group of children play on a frozen pond. Others are milling about in the street, both young and old alike. Four men are completing work on the wooden frame of a small building. Among the throng, by a cart in the street, a man leads a woman on a donkey. Only the telltale saw over his shoulder gives us a clue to his identity and that of his mounted companion.

Breugel's painting powerfully depicts how unnoticed the holy family were when they arrived in Bethlehem. If its inhabitants knew just who it was who needed a labour suite that evening, perhaps their response to the family would have been different.

A legend is told of how some angels attempted to clean up Bethlehem – physically and morally – for the birth of Jesus. They scrubbed and fumigated, and discussed how unsuitable a place Bethlehem was for such an event. When they had nearly completed their preparations, Gabriel put a stop to the work and ordered everything to be put back into its former condition. God had said, 'This is for real'.

That reality meant the holy family received a painful rejection from the inhabitants of Bethlehem. What a contrast: Mary had welcomed Jesus into her own body nine months previously; now he finds no welcome from the people of his birthplace.

And yet, as people went about their business in Bethlehem, God went about his. Jesus was by then only hours from arriving right in the midst of a people wrapped up in their own affairs.

God was about to demonstrate that his purpose and presence do not depend on those who take notice.

'. . . you did not recognise the time of God's coming to you' (Luke 19:44). These words, spoken over Jerusalem, could also have been applied some 30 years previously to Bethlehem when Jesus was born there. Both towns failed to offer a welcome fit for a king. But it wasn't just corporate rejection which Jesus faced. Our main reading shows us an important incident in the later life of Christ when an individual provided hospitality for him in a fashion which was far from warm.

Simon the Pharisee's invitation for Jesus to dine with him might have included good food, but was well short on social graces. No water to wash Jesus' feet, no welcoming gesture towards him, no oil for his head. But it was not just the outward lack of public etiquette which Jesus chose to highlight. The one who searches our hearts realised that Simon had misjudged him. 'If this man were a prophet, he would know . . .' was Simon's attitude towards Jesus. The Pharisee had summed up his visitor and found him wanting, in his opinion. In his dinner discourse, Jesus showed him pointedly that the welcoming love of a sinful woman was more valuable than the righteous judgements of a pious man. That love was the doorway to her heart through which forgiveness would flood.

The reason God can seem like a stranger is because we don't treat him like a guest. On 1 December we examined this whole issue of welcoming God by his Spirit into each area of our lives. Mary opened wide her very womb at the beginning of her pregnancy and allowed Jesus in. And here, at the very end of those nine months, the issue of welcome is still one to be confronted. But this time it is the inhabitants of Bethlehem who face the challenge; sadly they were found wanting. Providing God with a warm welcome in our lives is not just a once-for-all event. It is a conscious daily activity. We would not be considered much of a host if we welcomed friends into our house for a week, but only took notice of them for the first day. So it is with God. If we have allowed him into our lives, he should be made welcome all the time. After all, he is the perfect guest.

Prayer

O come, O come, Emmanuel,
you are welcome in my life.
Forgive me for the times I have failed to welcome you,
and so have forfeited that closeness with you.
Help me each day to open my life afresh to you.
Save me from the busyness which might cause me to miss you.
Amen.

24 DECEMBER

LABOUR PAINS

Readings: John 16:17-24; Romans 8:18-25

Now that their journey to Bethlehem was safely over, Mary and Joseph found themselves reflecting that the anticipation of it had in fact been worse than the reality. En route, they had passed other travellers, on their way to different towns for the census. They had greeted each other cordially, fellow pilgrims forced into temporary relocation by a Roman emperor. None of those they passed had realised they were witnessing the penultimate antenatal journey of the Son of God.

Mary had found it increasingly difficult to get comfortable, sitting on the donkey. The saddle was good enough, but the uneven surface of the road had made for a rough ride. She had tried shifting position every few minutes; relief had been short-lived. Over the previous week she had been feeling contractions – a sudden tightness in her abdomen – which she felt certain had increased in intensity and regularity as the bumpy donkey ride progressed.

Now her contractions seemed like the physical sighs of her heart's deepest longing – for Jesus to be born. They had gone through so much together, and now all Mary wanted to do was to hold him close in her arms; to see and feel this child who had been part of her own body for nine months. Each contraction was like a silent fanfare to Jesus' arrival. Mary knew it would not be long now before motherhood would begin for real.

The pain of childbirth signifies the imminent arrival of new life. Labour looks forward to birth, not backwards to conception. The pain is a major sign that the waiting is nearly over, that expectancy is soon to be rewarded.

Jesus used the image of childbirth to help his disciples under-stand how their grief at his death would turn into joy at his resurrection. His rising from the grave opened the way for us to enjoy eternal companionship with God in heaven. Jesus sought to encourage his disciples with this truth. 'And if I go and prepare a place for you, I will come back and take you to be with me that you also may be where I am' (John 14:3). The one who came at Christmas teaches us to long for the place he temporarily left behind.

This yearning for heaven is picked up by the writers of the New Testament. St Paul likens this longing of all creation to the groans of labour (Romans 8:22). In the chapter which recounts the stories of biblical heroes of faith, the author of the letter to the Hebrews paints a different picture of this yearning: 'They admitted that they were aliens and strangers on earth. People who say such things show that they are looking for a country of their own. If they had been thinking of the country they had left, they could have had opportunity to return. Instead, they were looking for a better country – a heavenly one' (Hebrews 11:13-16).

I love these images of longing for a better country. All our groanings of despair, disappointment, pain and loss in this life add up to one truth – we are longing for another place we can truly call home. We are waiting for a better existence in a land where we do not yet live. Like the prodigal son in Jesus' parable, coming to his senses far from home, we realise that though it may seem far away, we know where we would really like to be.

The season of Christmas provokes us to think about what we really desire. We find ourselves being asked, 'What would you like for Christmas?' When it comes to giving clues for presents, we can sometimes find ourselves exercising diplomatic restraint, since what we *really* want cannot be asked for.

Amongst the brightly wrapped parcels which represent, to some degree, a summary of what we desire on a material level, there lie unseen presents upon which we would long to find our name. These are the secret longings which no one will see this Christmas. They reside deep within us and are not for public view. They are the 'if onlys' of our hearts, the hopes and dreams we dare not whisper. They are the thoughts at the back of our minds, which surface even as we joyfully open our Christmas presents. Such hopes can be some of the most powerful forces within us, since, long after the wrapping paper has been torn to reveal our material gains at Christmases past, those dreams may still remain, still unfulfilled.

What do we *really* want this Christmas? What do we long for? Those things which perhaps seem so close, and have not yet come to birth? This Christmas is an opportunity to offer again those hopes to the God we remember as the giver of a unique gift. It is not easy to understand why some of our dreams still lie unrealised. We have seen this Advent how God's ways can so often surprise us. We can only stand and wonder again at the generosity of God, who did not withhold his own Son from us. Somehow, in this breathtaking act of lavishness, we must seek the security that God will not hold back from us anything he knows we truly need. 'He who did not spare his own Son, but gave him up for us all – how will he not also, along with him, graciously give us all things?' (Romans 8:32). And beyond those desires for the things of this life, let us foster our yearnings for heaven, that better country and a future home which will be the culmination of all we have been hoping for.

Prayer

O come, O come, Emmanuel,
the desire of nations,
and let me find this Christmas that, as the old carol says,
'The hopes and fears of all the years are met in thee'.
You know the secret longings of my heart,
the dreams I have but dare not share.
I offer these to you;
graciously sift them to leave only your will for me.
Grant me courage to lay aside the rest
and to take hold of what you desire for me.
Amen.

25 DECEMBER

THE WORD MADE FLESH

Reading: John 1:1-18

It was not long before Mary entered the final stages of labour. She had welcomed Jesus into her body; now, as a last antenatal act of co-operation with him, she had to push him through that short, but dangerous, journey along the birth canal and into the world. Joseph held and encouraged her, with fervent prayers muttered under his breath.

The innkeeper's wife had by this time joined them to assist at the birth. Joseph was relieved to have her there. A mother of three herself, she had recognised Mary's advanced state of labour as soon as she saw her. Having brought plenty of hot water and towels, and with an air of quiet confidence, she set about instructing Mary as the birth began. Little did the innkeeper's wife know who she was helping into the world.

Elsewhere on the earth, its inhabitants were unaware of this unprecedented spectacle. Yet in heaven it was as if all time had been suspended. And, as angels held their breath, Jesus finally slipped from Mary's body. The innkeeper's wife wiped some blood and mucus from the baby's face. A good, strong cry soon followed, so alien in that stable. The first sound of the incarnated Word. She passed Jesus to Joseph and dextrously tied two thin strips of cloth tightly around the umbilical cord as Deity was held in the palms of a manual labourer. 'I think you should cut the cord,' the innkeeper's wife said to Joseph. He passed Jesus to Mary who cradled him against her for the first time.

Quivering, Joseph knelt, the knife in his hand pressed against the umbilical cord. In all his years of carpentry, this was the most important cut he would ever make: Jesus released from the security of his attachment to Mary, history for ever divided into BC and AD. The world had received a very personal visit from its creator.

Next day, the innkeeper and his wife hastily ushered the family into a room vacated at breakfast. Mary sat up in bed, encouraging Jesus to feed. Lips from which all creation was spoken into being, which sustain it still, now searched instinctively for sustenance from a mother's breast.

Unable to settle, Joseph made his way to the census point and stood patiently in the queue, still lost in thought at all that had happened. Presently he reached the front of the queue.

'Name and home town?' barked the Roman official.

'Joseph, son of Jacob, from Nazareth.'

'Occupation?'

'Carpenter.'

'Any dependants?'

'Yes, a wife, and . . .' Joseph paused and, with pride, added, 'a son, just born.'

Joseph saw the official record both Mary's and Jesus' details alongside his on the parchment. Jesus – numbered as one of us. Emmanuel had truly come.

Above the door of a small hospital amidst the trenches of the First World War battlefields, a sign bore the inscription: 'Abandon all rank, ye who enter here.' Among the dead and the dying, status pales into insignificance. Injury and illness are great levellers.

That same sign could have been placed before Jesus as he prepared to enter the world. It was a place in which he would have to lay aside his title to meet people's deepest needs. God made himself subject to the human process of conception, pregnancy and birth. The inventor of life participated in his own invention. The invincible God, who holds the whole universe in his hands, allowed himself to be cradled in the arms of a teenage mother.

God had truly placed himself in our shoes. For a period of some 30 years, God would have a different perspective on human existence, all because he himself had become a human being.

The beauty of the prologue to John's Gospel captures these amazing truths. 'The Word became flesh and made his dwelling among us' (verse 14). In the original Greek, there is powerful imagery here: 'pitched his tent (tabernacled) among us' would be a truer rendering of the phrase. Distant images of God among his people in the tabernacle in the wilderness spring to mind. God was pitching his tent once more upon the earth. But this was no ordinary tent. Jesus was God's living tabernacle, a canvas of human skin stretched over a flesh-covered skeletal frame. The divine encased in humanity. A temporary living, breathing, talking, eating, sleeping, walking home on the earth for God. And, through that covering of humanity, the inner glory of heaven shone bright.

My wife and I recently had our first proper experience of camping. We had borrowed most of the necessary equipment and had received crash-course instructions in survival under canvas. Things began well, but it was only our second night when the heavens opened. Torrential rain hammered on the roof of the tent, thunder boomed overhead and lightning zigzagged with white brilliance around us as several large storms chased each other across the sky. It was several hours later, with the rain relentlessly falling, that we realised the wind was blowing rain in a fine spray through one side of the tent. Fumbling in the semi-darkness with extra plastic sheets, we hastily erected a makeshift screen inside the tent to keep the rain at bay. Mercifully no rain came through the roof, but with one side of our bedding wet, we slept very close to each other that night!

First light revealed a decidedly sodden group of individuals with not much in their tents that had escaped a soaking. It was clear we had all had a bad night; even the seasoned campers among us remarked that it had been the worst night of camping they had experienced. Yet the level of understanding and helpfulness which abounded that morning was just what we needed to keep us going. Three cheers for the solidarity of campers!

When I think back to that time, it helps me, in a small way, to remember how Jesus 'pitched his tent among us'. His solidarity with us was total; his commitment exemplary. The campsite he chose was not particularly attractive; it was full of need and hurting badly. Yet he did not shun this darkness. In fact, he came into the midst of it, the very thing which would neither understand, nor overcome him.

Expecting Jesus – that is what Christmas is about. Expecting him to be close, whatever circumstances we face in life. And the manner in which he came among us that first Christmas shows that our expectation of his presence is not wild fantasy. Our hope is based on a God who came so close inside a mother's body that he felt the very heartbeat of humanity. A God who comes that near has shown his commitment to be with us, just as Jesus said, 'to the very end of the age'.

This book scratches only the surface of the rich soil that is Christmas. Yet I pray that this December you have come to expect Jesus to be close in fresh ways. Amidst the presents you will open today, God gives us his precious gift of Jesus, our Emmanuel. And, long after the other gifts have faded into irrelevance and disuse, Jesus will still walk beside us, an ever-present companion through all of our lives.

Prayer

O come, O come, Emmanuel,
I rejoice today in your birth.
Thank you that you came among us as one of us,
the final Word on life.
And now, as you lived in Mary,
live in me and spread your love through me.
My hands can be your hands,
my words can be your words.
Help me to expect you not only to be with me,
but to do great things through me,
for your glory.
Amen.

TAKING THINGS FURTHER

Summary

The months leading up to Jesus' birth became busier and busier for Mary and Joseph. It was as if these last weeks had quietly crept up and taken them by surprise. Where had the previous six months gone? The time for the birth was nearly upon them. From the moment Gabriel had announced God's plan to Mary, she and Joseph knew their lives would never be the same again. But now, on the threshold of the birth, this fact seemed more real than ever. Big decisions were facing the holy couple and their experiences in this third trimester raise for us issues of how we take decisions and what the Lord's involvement is in that process.

So it was that the holy couple packed what they could on a donkey and made for Bethlehem. It was as difficult as they had imagined it to be. Mary could find no comfort on the donkey and was exhausted by the end of each day's travel. So many changes in so short a space of time. As we travel with Mary and Joseph on their journey to Bethlehem, we consider how we respond to times of change in our own lives. How does our faith in an unchanging God help us to cope with times of transition?

Whatever relief Mary felt on arrival at Bethlehem was soon overtaken by the pains of labour. The next hours are known so well in history, yet shrouded in holy secrecy, too. By the end of that night, in the stable of an inn, God squeezed himself into the world from Mary's contracting womb. Few people witnessed this incredible spectacle or its immediate aftermath. But centuries of time have not tempered the wonder of that moment. God had come closer than ever before.

Discussion questions

17. What are the signs that Jesus is being placed first in a particular area of our lives? What helps us to keep him first?

18. Using a concordance, make a study of the word 'wait' in the Bible. What insights do you gain about reliance on the Lord during a period of waiting?

19. In what ways can you nurture your faith, a) as an individual and b) through a small fellowship group? Could you create further opportunities for sharing how you are growing in faith in your group?

20. How do you respond to times of change? What are the benefits and difficulties of such times? How can you welcome the Lord's presence into these situations?

21. In what ways can God guide us into the future? What has your experience been so far? How might you deepen your trust in the God who goes before you?

22. What particular frustrations do you think Jesus experienced during his time on earth? Bring to the Lord any frustrations in your own life, situations where no progress is being made. What do you sense the Lord wants to say to you about this?

23. Take some time to think about the activities in your life. How busy are you and how far is God involved in your pursuits?

24. 'What do you *really* want for Christmas?' Try to answer this question as honestly as you can.

25. John describes Jesus as 'The Word'. Why do you think he used this phrase? What was Jesus seeking to communicate about God and humankind?

POST-CHRISTMAS
READINGS
26-31 DECEMBER

26 DECEMBER

UNEXPECTED GUESTS

Reading: Luke 2:8-20

A profound sense of peace had descended upon the stable, blanketing the holy family in a strange but welcome warmth. The anguish of the labour was past; now wonder shone in the eyes of Mary and Joseph. Jesus had had his first feed. For now it had been adequate; both mother and son were learning a new art. But the journey from womb to world is tiring indeed, and even the human eyes of God could not fight sleep. And so, resting in the manger, the infant Christ was adored by Mary and Joseph.

There was a sudden scuffling sound and muffled voices outside the stable door. Then it creaked slightly open and a wind-worn, bearded face peered round. When they looked back to that night, Mary and Joseph could not remember the opening words that passed between them and those shepherds, but before they knew it, the stable seemed to be full of them, and not a few sheep as well. They swarmed round the manger, like bees round a honey pot, and stood or knelt in silent awe. Jesus remained asleep, but that did not seem to matter to them. This weather-beaten band of shepherds had found the Christ of whom angels had spoken.

The Christmas story is full of surprises. The shepherds had to be the most unlikely visitors that could ever have been predicted for the new-born Messiah. That night they went from sheep-watching to baby-watching. They learned for the first time that an animal's feeding trough can double as a cradle when there's nothing else available.

When parents rejoice at the birth of a child, whom do they tell first? Often it will be close relatives, then special friends. Birth announcements are sent eventually to a wider circle of acquaintances. On the night God's Son was born, there were only two announcements: from angels in the sky to a bunch of shepherds and via a star in the sky to a group of magi. What a strange choice! God was definitely breaking with birth protocol.

The shepherds were humble people who received the news unquestioningly. They became the first investigative detectives in the AD period of history, tracking down the location of the baby in the manger. They also became the first evangelists, spreading news of his arrival to the people of the area.

Like an unknown artist visiting just after the birth of Picasso, or an unsung composer cooing over baby Mozart, so those shepherds looked into the infant eyes of the Good Shepherd. In that close encounter with Jesus they did not realise they were meeting with their future role model. It was his voice, just an unintelligible cooing then, which would one day claim to be the voice which all his followers knew and understood. As that Good Shepherd, he would enter by the gate and call each of his sheep by name. And having led them out, he would go ahead of them. This Shepherd would be like no other, voluntarily laying down his life for his sheep.

We do not know how old those shepherds were who came to visit the infant Christ that glorious night. But I imagine there were some among them who were young enough still to be alive when Jesus began his public ministry. And I wonder if any of them heard that great speech about him being the Good Shepherd and wondered just what kind of man this was. If they did, would they have successfully deduced that the man who spoke like this was once that baby they had seen in the manger? And would their hearts have so warmed to this man that they became his followers – shepherds becoming like sheep?

God has a habit of turning people's lives upside down. Just like those shepherds who perhaps became sheep in the fold of Christ. Just like Saul of Tarsus, who went from persecutor to proclaimer. Just like Zacchaeus, whose greed was turned into generosity. Just like Simon Peter, a fisher of fish, then a fisher of men.

Those who are changed by Christ should become story-tellers for him. Stories of what he has done in our life, true tales of how relationship with him has made a difference to us. Even those uneducated shepherds lost no time in spreading the news of their nocturnal discovery in that Bethlehem stable.

Look carefully into the opening chapters of Matthew's and Luke's Gospels and you will observe the spreading of news and the curiosity of those who receive it. But there were no trained preachers operating to propagate the glad tidings. Those who spoke of those marvellous events were all ordinary people who had simply become caught up in the dealings of an extraordinary God. It was all word of mouth. People speaking of what they had seen and heard. Personal testimony that couldn't be kept a secret.

Christmas is a time for stories. On our shelves my wife and I have a book of thirty Christmas stories. I use the word 'Christmas' because that is how they are described. They are in fact stories set in or around the Christmas period. There is, of course, only one Christmas story. And sadly there will be many people this Christmas who will enjoy many stories but never hear the one which really matters. Who will ensure that the original script does not get lost? We may look to those we consider the 'professionals' – the ministers, the evangelists – to do this job. But we will miss the point if we do. The real Christmas story draws people like no other. It is not just a story to be enjoyed by children. It contains powerful truths about the nature of our lives and God's response. It is a story through which people may encounter the main character for the very first time, not as the baby in the manger, but as the Saviour and Lord who seeks our discipleship. And we who have already yielded to that Lord are the very ones who should speak of him and his story to the world he came to save.

Prayer

O come, O come, Emmanuel,
and let me again enjoy the one story this Christmas
which really matters.
Let me savour the story of the Saviour.
May the implications of this story not lie dormant within me,
but stir me as you did those shepherds of old,
to speak of what I've seen and heard –
that same Christmas story which has touched my life too.
Amen.

27 DECEMBER

OUT INTO THE OPEN

Reading: Luke 2:18-39

He'd been waiting, anticipating a moment of such fulfilment it would complete his life. And so, over the years since the Holy Spirit had revealed that his eyes would see the Messiah, he had prayed in expectation . . . and waited, each day holding the potential of promise.

And then it came again, that unmistakable inner voice of promise, that was now a voice of fulfilment. This was the day. And so it was that Simeon stepped from his Jerusalem home, with heart thumping and butterflies fluttering in his stomach, and headed for the temple. What did he expect to see? He was not sure; he only knew that the Spirit would show him when the time came.

Oblivious to the people around him, he made his way through the streets. Although fully in control of all his faculties, he felt swept along by a mighty tide of heaven. His years of waiting would soon be over.

Passing through the temple's outer gateway, he came into the outer courts. He stood, quivering, with eyes bright and alert, his spirit quickened by years of faithful prayer. He was motionless for a while, scanning the milling crowds who were there with their offerings. Suddenly, Simeon's gaze alighted upon a young couple. There was nothing remarkable about them at first glance: the wife carried a baby in her arms, the husband held a small cage with two pigeons. They had come for the ceremony of purification after childbirth.

Simeon could not take his eyes off the child. There was an aura, a presence from the infant that left Simeon in no doubt: this was the object of his quest. The young couple had already reached the priest by the time Simeon came up to them. When Mary and Joseph thought back to that time, they remembered a kindly looking old man who asked if he might hold their son. It was only when he started to speak that they realised they were in the presence of a prophet. His words were so strikingly clear that Mary never forgot them: words of promise, salvation, hope. And Mary still remembered the shiver down her spine as Simeon spoke of a sword to pierce her heart. It was the last thing she recalled him saying.

And Simeon, after cradling salvation in his arms, gave Jesus back to Mary, smiled lovingly at her and turned to leave. Sighing in deep satisfaction, he made his way back home, oblivious once more to those around him, to die in peace.

According to the Law of Moses (Leviticus 12), Mary and Joseph would have brought Jesus to the temple when he was six weeks old. This incident is the first recorded time that Jesus was brought out in public for his identity to be revealed. The Saviour who had been hidden for so long was now coming out into the open. But on that special day in Jerusalem, only four people knew that Jesus had been there: the two who brought him and the two who blessed him. For everyone else, this was just another day at the temple. The sacrifices went on as usual, the ceremony continued, the priests went about their duties.

Jesus was too young that day to take notice of much. But 30 years later he would be back and all the city would know. For in those very same temple courts where Jesus was presented as an infant he would, as an adult, drive out money-changers with a whip of cords, challenging the very core of the Jewish faith. That put him on a fatal collision course with the Jewish leaders. They thought they had rid Israel of a blaspheming troublemaker when they watched Jesus trudge to Golgotha, but within hours, back at that same temple, the curtain shielding the Holy of Holies would be torn in two, to show that Jesus was a man who would not be silenced.

Simeon was given a privileged glimpse into something of this destiny. He was shown that God's plan of salvation was to encompass more than just the Jewish nation, and that the little boy he held in his arms was the key to it all. Simeon saw the divisive nature of Jesus' future ministry, which probed so deeply to expose the rotten core of hypocritical religion. I would say that Simeon sensed that with Jesus you would either be with him or against him. This child would grow to be a man who allowed no middle ground. I wonder if Simeon knew just how brutally the sword he saw would have to strike – for both Mary and Jesus. The price of the salvation over which Simeon rejoiced was high indeed.

I am deeply humbled when I read of Simeon. He represents some-thing of what I would wish to be when I am old. As I contemplate his character I am awed at the privilege that Simeon, out of all the people in Jerusalem, was granted that day. For me to hold my own son is wonder enough, but Simeon cradling God as a helpless infant is a greater marvel. But the privilege was the reward for constant expectation. Mary and Joseph had been expecting Jesus for nine months prior to meeting him. Although the text does not specify how long Simeon waited to see Jesus, I have a sneaking suspicion it was many years. So when Mary and Joseph met Simeon, they were learning lessons of their own about how to be expectant about God. Here was a man whose attitude to God was one of such openness that he moved only and always at his Lord's bidding. For those aspiring to be like him, I see five qualities to pray for in our lives.

First of all, if we are to be open to the Lord's presence, we must be righteous. This cannot come of ourselves, but by faith in God's grace. The forgiveness Jesus won reaches sinners like you and me. Secondly, Luke records that Simeon was known to be devout. There was a personal commitment in him to pursue holiness. I have a sense that no one could catch Simeon in sin. That is not to say he was sinless, but that he lived carefully within the requirements of godliness. Conscious of my own failings, I know I have far to go to be as Simeon was. The Holy Spirit played a strong role in this man's life. The other three qualities I see in Simeon are that he was touched by the Spirit, he received from the Spirit and he was moved by the Spirit. Here was a man in communion with God regularly through the Holy Spirit. When I consider the level of insight Simeon received, I am drawn all the more to welcome the work of the Spirit in me.

Simeon shines as an example to us all. He encourages us to be people who see the Lord in a world which does not look for him. He challenges us to speak with divine revelation to make known God's purposes. Each of our moments is unique and priceless. When I hold my baby son, I think of Simeon cradling the infant Christ. Every time I hold Thomas I realise I will never have that particular moment again. Simeon, too, could never have that moment with Jesus again. But because of his expectancy, he didn't need a replay. He was satisfied completely, and for Simeon a great promise now beckoned him to the place where he could be with his God for ever.

Prayer

O come, O come, Emmanuel,
the promised Messiah from ancient times.
Grant me the expectancy of Simeon
to await your intervention on my behalf.
Cause me to pursue holiness as a way of life,
fashioned in me by your Spirit.
Cause me to seek openness to your leading,
prompted by the voice of your Spirit.
Help me to see your purposes being worked out in the world,
that I may play my part in all you are doing.
Amen.

28 DECEMBER

THE FRAGRANCE OF CHRISTMAS

Reading: Matthew 2:1-12

The weeks immediately following Jesus' birth were filled with many important decisions for Mary and Joseph. One such decision forced upon them was where to make their home. Knowing they would have to present Jesus at the temple at six weeks of age, Mary and Joseph saw little point in returning to Nazareth, only to make the long journey back south to Jerusalem, when Bethlehem was only five miles away from that great city.

Joseph therefore spent his early days of fatherhood visiting the workshops of Bethlehem's carpenters, seeking temporary work. The trade of the woodworker seemed to be in demand in the town, and Joseph was successful in securing employment in a workshop near the synagogue. In time, Mary and Joseph found a small house to rent, and decided to settle in Bethlehem until Jesus was older. So life for the holy family went on.

Mary and Joseph never forgot the night the magi came. Jesus was nearly two by then. Darkness was falling, when the noise of voices and animals in the street disrupted the evening peace. The fine detail of what followed was a blur to Joseph when, years later, he brought that night to mind. But the camels, flowing robes, neatly cut beards, foreign accents and expensive gifts were the tiles that formed the mosaic of that moment. The visitors did not stay long, but time seemed suspended as those gracious guests poured out their adoration to Jesus. It seemed to Joseph that the fragrance of the frankincense they offered was the very perfume of that first Christmas night. Memories of the birth came flooding back to him: the wonder of watching Jesus slip into the world. Time had moved on so quickly since then – the tiny new-born had fleshed out, the baby was fast becoming a toddler. The gift of the magi had re-awakened memories of that first extraor-dinary night.

Joseph stood just outside the threshold as he bid farewell to their unexpected visitors, their silhouetted forms melting into the darkness. He almost felt the need to pinch himself to check he had not imagined them, especially in the light of his previous vivid dreams. But the incense flask in his hands was proof enough of the reality of the guests. Was there no end to the surprises associated with this child? Joseph smiled to himself and looked into the night sky, where a bright star directly overhead seemed to twinkle back at him.

It doesn't take much for the spirit of Christmas to fade. No sooner has Boxing Day come, than thoughts inevitably turn to the New Year. And 1 January seems an annual watershed, cutting us off from the Christmas just past. For many, Christmas is such a difficult time that it is something to be 'got over and done with'. We all need ways of keeping the true spirit and message of Christmas alive throughout the whole year.

The story of the magi can help us to do just that. They brought back to Mary and Joseph the wonder of the early days with Jesus. The Gospel writers leave us to speculate on what the holy family did in the months which followed Jesus' birth. Matthew's account sees the magi searching and finding the infant Christ in Bethlehem. But Herod's edict to kill all the firstborn sons there under two years old must have meant that Jesus was approaching that age. We can only guess that the holy family remained for a time in the place of Jesus' birth. And so it was that these strange travellers came to find a baby boy so far from their own home.

Never in their wildest dreams would Mary and Joseph have anticipated such visitors, and how unexpected were their gifts! Certainly not standard presents to celebrate a baby's birth! Yet, because these gifts are so unusual and from such fascinating donors, they have a powerful story to tell. Today and for the next two days we will be reflecting on the gifts the magi brought. They represent attitudes we can hold to help us be open to the Lord's presence. The magi are examples of those who saw that the birth of this child had long-term implications. This had been no ordinary nativity. Though they did not fully realise it at the time, history was being rewritten, the whole calendar of the world was being reset. They did, however, recognise that an important event had occurred and the gifts they brought reflected this.

The increasing secularisation of society has drained Christmas not only of its real meaning but also its true spirit. The hype of consumerism can whip people into a frenzy in December, but drops them down with a thump come January. In this environment, even Christians find that the message of Christmas wanes in their lives within days of 25 December. I am shocked at the way I have caught myself continuing with my life, as if I have packed Jesus away with the unwanted presents. This has not been a conscious decision on my part to shut him out. Instead, a subtle dilution of the good news of Christmas has taken place within me. The story of the magi and the incense they brought have inspired me to see that things can be different.

The magi were seers and seekers. Not content to see a particular star, they had to discover the origin of its appearance and track its movements all the way to the young Christ. They were looking for signs of God's presence in the world. Throughout the days of their long journey from the East to Bethlehem, the incense they carried was like the fragrance of Christmas, a constant reminder of the purpose of their pilgrimage, particularly as the weeks went by.

As I consider my desire for the spirit of Christmas to fill my heart all the year round, I know that my attitude must be that of the magi. They steadfastly sought after Jesus, desiring to worship him. That attitude brought them face-to-face with Jesus. The King was then close and, as the magi went back home, they carried Jesus' presence with them in their hearts. He was then forever close.

And what of Mary and Joseph? The magi's visit was equally significant for them. The gifts the exotic strangers left were tokens of a precious day. No child more important would ever be born. No birthday would be more celebrated. Caught up in the everyday pressures of parenting, it was vital for them not to lose touch with the memory of those early days. And how important those gifts would prove to be when the holy family were forced into exile in Egypt. Stripped of their home, their friends, their country, the scent of the incense they carried would have been a powerful reminder of who they were and where they belonged.

We, too, will carry the fragrance of Christmas with us, as we realise just how close Christ is at all times of the year. For those, like the magi, who see and seek, every day is a Christ-filled day.

Prayer

O come, O come, Emmanuel,
and fill my heart with the fragrance of Christmas,
that precious perfume
of the appreciation of your presence.
Grant me the eyes of the Magi to see
and their perseverance to seek after you
every day of my pilgrimage.
Help me to carry that fragrance in my heart all year.
May its potency not fade as Christmas passes,
but instead the beauty of its scent so diffuse around me
that others are drawn into your sweet embrace.
Amen.

29 DECEMBER

COUNTING THE COST

OF CHRISTMAS

Reading: Ephesians 2:11–22

A strangely awed silence fell as one of the magi opened his flask and the scent of myrrh filled the room. Myrrh was well known to both Mary and Joseph who had experienced its odour in the embalming of the dead. But what an incongruous gift to give in celebration of a birth! What had this visitor in mind?

Mary's mind suddenly flashed back to the words of Simeon in the temple: 'And a sword will pierce your own soul.' Was there a connection? She could not be sure.

At first he did not know why, but Joseph found himself thinking back to his anticipation of the birth of Jesus, and how he had tried to have confidence in his role as birth assistant. This was not a role he had expected to play and, with no rehearsal in prospect, he was a little unsure of how he would cope.

One thing which particularly embarrassed him when he thought ahead to the birth was that he might not cope with seeing the blood. Generally he would not have described himself as being squeamish, and there had been many occasions in his life as a carpenter when a misdirected nail or chisel had sent him running for a bandage. But seeing his own blood was somehow a different matter to dealing with someone else's. He had dreaded the thought of going weak at the knees and ending up on the floor with his head spinning. All at the time when he was supposed to be strong for Mary!

Joseph stared at the flask of myrrh on the table and pursued his thoughts in the uneasy silence which prevailed. Suddenly he saw a connection between his musings and the myrrh. It was the link between blood and sacrifice, something well known to every Jew. But what relation it bore to Jesus still puzzled him.

Joseph would indeed have witnessed the blood at Jesus' birth. We do not know how well he managed, but clearly all turned out well in the end. Yet Joseph was spared the trauma of witnessing a more horrific spectacle – the crucifixion of his own son. Mary did not escape this shocking sight. Not only did she witness the blood at Jesus' birth, but also the blood at his death. For we cannot speak of Christmas without speaking of Easter. The magi's gift of myrrh underlines this for us. That night in Bethlehem Mary shed her blood to bring Jesus' life into the world. She did not know then that he would in turn shed his own blood, not only for her, but also for the whole world.

Mary was the mother of a mediator, born to bring peace and reconciliation between God and humankind. Our reading from Ephesians dramatically describes our condition, which necessitated the coming of Christ. We were a people separate from him, without

God and devoid of hope. We were denied membership of God's family. Like foreigners excluded from citizenship, we possessed no passport to promise. What made the difference to this miserable state? It was the blood of Christ (verse 13) which brought us peace and proximity to God our Father.

It was a costly way to bring us this peace. Yet it was the only way. The shadow of the cross fell across Jesus even as he lay in Bethlehem's manger. The scent of myrrh, the smell of death, hung about him from the moment it was presented to him by the magi. Did he smell its pungent aroma in the sponge offered to him as a weak anaesthetic while he hung on the cross? Even in death its scent seeped around his shrouded, anointed body as he lay in the tomb.

The cross was a costly exercise in salvation. The cries of the infant king would one day turn into the agonising cries of the crucified Christ. His head, tinged with blood at his birth, would one day drip blood from the wounds of wild thorns. Calvary was the piercing of a son's body and a mother's soul. Through its violence would come peace to satisfy the wrath of a righteous God towards sin.

This December let us remember the true cost of Jesus coming near. For us, the cost of Christmas is measured by the size of hole in our bank account or the heightening of our blood pressure through encounters with relatives as difficult as they are distant. The cost of Christ's Christmas was the cross. It is time to pause in thankfulness that Jesus was prepared to pay that ultimate price.

The significance of Christmas can wane for us each year if we do not actively remember its meaning. For Jesus each birthday he celebrated brought him one year closer to the cross, one year nearer to his goal.

Let us rejoice in the rewards of Christ's obedience in coming at Christmas. Through his completed earthly mission, he won for us the right to change identity – no longer foreigners, but citizens of his kingdom; no longer outsiders, but full members of his family. The blood of the cross has provided our passport; it has bought our adoption papers.

We know we are getting close to someone when they demonstrate love in a poignant way. This December, don't forget the shadow of the cross falling across the crib; rejoice in the Saviour who showed the ultimate act of love, by dying for us to bring us close to him.

Prayer

O come, O come, Emmanuel,
and help me to realise the true cost of Christmas;
not the expense of presents or visits to relations,
but your blood shed for a broken world.
Help me to remember the cross this Christmas,
for that is why you came.
Thank you that you set your face to that goal
and paid the ultimate price.
Amen.

30 DECEMBER

WHAT'S IT ALL WORTH?

Reading: 1 Peter 1:3-14

Parenting had brought its unique demands to Mary and Joseph. Just because they were guardians to the Son of God did not exempt them from the normal responsibilities of parenthood. There were the sleepless nights, the added chores of washing and changing. There were the moments spent agonising over the reasons for a crying baby. There were the guilt trips over mistakes made and the possible damage done to the infant Jesus. The fact that the Son of God was under their care only heightened their anxiety.

During the pregnancy friends had said to them, 'There will be moments when you'll wonder if it's really all worth it and other times when you'll know it is worth it.' Mary and Joseph had found this to be true. In the early days there were moments during feeding sessions in the middle of the night when Mary had wondered if she had the energy to go on. Her life seemed only to consist of feeding and washing. But at many other times she had looked into the face of her sleeping son and been so overwhelmed with love and wonder that she would not have wanted her life to be any different.

The visit of the magi brought issues of worth back again to the forefront of their minds. Mary and Joseph were amazed at the commitment of these foreign men who had risked so much, just to honour their son. When the final gift was presented, Mary and Joseph gasped audibly. A small intricate casket lay open, brimming with gold coins. Only in the temple in Jerusalem had they seen more gold than this. Being shy and awkward about such things, Joseph had wondered about protesting: 'No, we couldn't possibly accept this', but then fell silent. For he realised that this was not about him at all. He was only a minor supporting player in an epic drama; there was only one person on whom the spotlight fell. Joseph looked again at the casket of gold and was speechless. For he knew that all the gold in the world would not be enough to express the worth of their son.

Every now and then we are tested by the big questions of life. Christians are not immune to the struggles these questions create. In fact, Christian belief forces us to consider questions that others would not. 'Is my faith worth it?' is one such question. The need for a sense of value in what we believe is strong in us all; we only thrive with meaning and purpose. It is not uncommon to find ourselves in situations where, at first glance, our faith seems pointless. Sometimes we feel caught in the slow lane of faith, sending rather jealous glances at others who seem more dynamic or favoured, speeding ahead of us. We wish that somehow our lives had more sparkle. Spare a thought, though, for those in the fast lane of faith, who may not be enjoying the experience as much as others think. They may have been sucked into one Christian activity after another until what matters most is what they do rather than what they believe. And when this happens, something is wrong.

Christmas clarifies the worth of our faith. It tells of a God who did not leave our world without hope of change, but entered it himself as a catalyst for renewal. Christmas tells us that sin will not have dominion for ever, because a sinless child would grow up and break its power. Is faith in Christ worth it? Christmas says a resounding, 'Yes!' to that question. And all because of what God has done. The true worth of our faith lies in the child who came at Christmas. The benefits he won for us during his life on earth have eternal worth. God's initiative sets the scene, our response completes the picture.

What will our response be this Christmas? Over the last 30 days we have taken privileged glimpses into the lives of those who were expecting Jesus. Today we view how the openness of the magi resulted in a lavish response to the one they sought. If we had asked them, 'Was your journey worth it?' they would have replied in the affirmative. We would, I believe, have still received a positive response had we questioned them earlier on: 'How's the trip going? Is it worth going on?' These men were resolute in pursuing their goal, passionate in their pilgrimage. The journey was long, they may have faced numerous dangers en route. But I don't believe they would ever have turned back. They knew who they wanted to be close to, and they knew he was a king. They came to worship and the worship they gave was worth more than the gold.

I have no gold to give the Lord, but I have a heart that he

considers is worth more. That heart is never perfect, sometimes broken, often sinful. It is fickle more than faithful. But God desires it as the best offering I can give. It doesn't matter what state it is in. As someone once said, 'God doesn't mind broken hearts, if we give him all the pieces.'

The problem is that we don't give him all the pieces. We keep bits back, thinking mistakenly that he either won't receive them, or that perhaps we could do our own patch-up job on them to make them respectable again. But the human heart doesn't mend like that. It finds its peace and rest only in relationship with the Father who made us. And entering that relationship means giving our whole heart to him, however many pieces, whatever the extent of the brokenness.

When I look back on my life and reflect upon the healing I have received through my relationship with Christ, I, too, must give an emphatic, 'Yes,' to the question, 'Is your faith worth it?' As we reflect upon the lavishness of the magi's gift of gold this Christmas, we have a fresh opportunity to consider the state of our hearts, and offer them again to their maker. For he is the Lord whose worth is endless.

Prayer

O come, O come, Emmanuel,
Lord of all, maker of heaven and earth.
Come visit the brokenness that is my heart,
and with tender hands grant healing.
Help me to offer you my whole heart,
A lavish gift, like that of the magi.
Help me to see that my pilgrimage, like theirs,
is worth every step.
Encourage me through your kindness
to see all the good you can do with my heart
if only I give you all the pieces.
Amen.

31 DECEMBER

THE FINAL WORD

Reading: Matthew 2:13-18

Joseph shot upright in the darkness, a small globule of sweat trickling down his neck. For a minute he sat motionless and silent, save for his short gasps of breath. He had to be certain he wasn't hearing things. Since his early days of parenting, both he and Mary listened so attentively for Jesus' cries that on some occasions they thought they heard sounds that simply weren't there. Joseph could therefore take no chances. But the more he re-played the dream, the more he was convinced of its authenticity. This was not the first time that angelic messengers had inhabited his dreams. Joseph knew an angel when he heard one. He turned and woke his sleeping wife. 'We have to go,' were his only words.

Calmly but quickly the couple gathered what possessions and provisions they could fit into saddlebags and loaded up the donkey. Only at the very last moment did they return to carry their sleeping toddler out to the stable. Joseph pulled up the door noiselessly behind him. They would never return. With Jesus cradled in Mary's arms on the donkey, Joseph glanced furtively round the stable door, to left and right, then led them out into the street. Quietly they made their way out of the town, Joseph's lantern their guide.

Memories of their enforced journey to Bethlehem for the census came flooding back. An unexpected journey to Bethlehem had now turned into an unexpected flight from the same town. It was all so hard to understand. Just when everything was beginning to settle down . . .

But they knew that there was no time to stand and ponder if Joseph's dream were true. This was a journey on which their very lives depended. And so the little family pressed on into the night, further and further from the town where so much had happened to them.

It was only hours later, in their wake, that Herod's soldiers moved in. Joseph's swift response ensured that the holy family never heard the screams of Bethlehem's mothers, which continued long and piercing into the night.

Of all the endings one might have predicted for the Christmas story, this would certainly not be it. Just as we are expecting an 'And they all lived happily ever after' conclusion, there is instead a brutal twist in the tale: the callous massacre of innocent children. It is a shocking and unpalatable episode. The morning after Joseph's dream found a family in exile and a town in mourning. How readily we remember Bethlehem for the birth of the Saviour; how much pleasanter it would be if we could forget that it was also the scene of so many babies' deaths. As the father of a young son myself, the events of that night do not bear thought.

We are left wondering what to make of it all. The holy family was being driven into exile. A Roman emperor's decree had summoned them to Bethlehem; now an edict from his puppet king was driving them from there. Was this God's idea of a happy ending?

And yet, Matthew's narrative does not end on a note of desolation. He brings his deep knowledge of ancient scripture to bear to remind us that this incident does not represent any change to the original script. Spoken through the lips and written by the quills of the prophets Jeremiah and Hosea centuries earlier, this exile is all part of God's plan. No one is stealing the script or rewriting the story. God, with his Living Word, is having the final word.

Some years back, as part of a job interview, I had to sit a psycho-metric test to see what kind of a person I am. One of the characteristics it identified (to no surprise of mine) is that I am a 'Completer/Finisher'. In other words, I am someone who works with fine detail and loves to tie up loose ends. This is true both in my work and personal life. It is probably in the latter that I find it hardest to live with loose ends. I like too much to have everything neatly sewn up and sorted out. If I find a loose end, I'm desperate to discover its missing partner, that I might tie the two together.

The slaughter of the innocents is the great loose end in the Christmas story. In such a beautiful narrative it is a jarring interruption. The holy family had to live with the reality of that massacre as an unresolved tension in their lives. Perhaps they struggled with guilt for being the cause of so great a loss of life. Did they even know some of the children who had died, having lived for a time in Bethlehem?

I am discovering that it is not always possible to tie up the loose ends in my life, no matter how much I want this to happen. The resolution of some circumstances is no longer within my control. I have done all I can. The matter is now in the Lord's hands. I find it easier to leave it with the Lord when I remember that it is he who is writing the script. The Lord who is the final Word will not abandon me to a fate determined by someone else. As I trust him, he will continue to work out his purposes in my life. Because he is in charge of the climax, I can trust him when the plot is not as tidy as I would like.

I hope that this Christmas you have discovered just how close Christ really is. I hope you have been able to welcome him into the circumstances you are currently facing. You will find him a dependable companion. Christmas revealed him as the Word; he will have the final say in our lives, if we truly let him. In many ways, all of our lives on earth are unfinished business, because the desire of our God is to take us to a world beyond and better than the only one we know. So let us continue to trust him and call him close in all our situations, knowing that for us who believe, a new world will one day beckon, where his presence will be fully revealed and his glory will never fade.

rayer

O come, O come, Emmanuel,
the Living Word,
be the final Word in my life.
Help me not to fear the loose ends that dangle in my life.
Grant me the patience to live with them,
offering them to you,
and knowing that you may choose to resolve some of them
in your way and in your time.
Thank you again for the message of Christmas,
for the expectation that Christ will be with me in all circumstances.
Step through the threshold of this New Year with me,
And may I openly welcome you
and see you at work in me in the months which follow
and in all the years ahead,
until you welcome me at last into the place
where I'll see your presence like never before.
Amen.

POST-CHRISTMAS

TAKING THINGS FURTHER

Summary

Mary and Joseph were soon swept into the responsibilities of parenthood. No amount of practical preparation had quite helped them with the immediate decisions that had to be made with a newborn baby. It was hard in the early days, being so far from home, but visits from kindly shepherds, encouragement from saintly prophets like Simeon and later gifts from wise men all combined to prolong the wonder of Jesus' birth. And for us, this is an important lesson. How quickly the events of Christmas can fade as we move into the New Year. The post-Christmas events we read of in scripture encourage us to find ways of carrying the fragrance of Christmas with us throughout the whole year.

Mary and Joseph needed this encouragement because within two years of Jesus' birth they were driven to flee for their lives into Egypt, thus escaping a terrible slaughter of young boys in Bethlehem. This might have seemed such a wrong conclusion to the Christmas tale, yet God was still in control. His purposes were wrapped up in all that was happening. The closing events of the Christmas story point us to the God who is the final word in our lives. A New Year is a good occasion to reflect upon what his sovereignty in our lives really means. What will it mean for us to place him first in this New Year?

Discussion questions

26. In a group, share together what each person loves most about the Christmas story. Enjoy what each person shares. Then turn your thoughts into prayers of thanks. If you are on

your own, read the Christmas narratives in Matthew and Luke in one sitting. What strikes you most?

27. Look at the five qualities of Simeon mentioned in the text. How can we encourage each of these to take firmer root in our lives?

28. What makes it so easy for the message of Christmas to fade? In what ways could we keep it alive throughout the year?

29. Think about what Jesus gave up to be born among us. Give thanks for the price he was prepared to pay.

30. Identify what in your life makes faith in Christ worthwhile. Write your answers down and keep them in your Bible, to encourage you when life is difficult.

31. What encouragement does it give you to know that Jesus is the final Word on your life?